FORAGED & RECYCLED ART

FORAGED & RECYCLED ART

35 PROJECTS MADE FROM FOUND, NATURAL, AND REPURPOSED MATERIALS

CLARE YOUNGS

CICO BOOKS

LONDON NEW YORK

Published in 2023 by CICO Books

An imprint of Ryland Peters & Small Ltd

20–21 Jockey's Fields   341 E 116th St

London WC1R 4BW   New York, NY 10029

www.rylandpeters.com

10 9 8 7 6 5 4 3 2 1

ISBN: 978-1-80065-207-1

Printed in China

Editors: Katie Hardwicke, Anna Southgate, Clare Sayer

Designer: Geoff Borin

Photographers: Caroline Arber: pages 90–91, 116–117;
Claire Richardson: pages 72–74, 86–88; Joanna Henderson:
pages 10–23, 26–35, 43–51, 54–59, 63–64, 69–71, 77–79, 97–107,
113, 115; James Gardiner: pages 24, 37, 52–53, 60–61, 65–66,
80–83, 108–111

Styling: Clare Youngs

Illustration: Clare and Ian Youngs

In-house editor: Jenny Dye
Art director: Sally Powell
Creative director: Leslie Harrington
Head of production: Patricia Harrington
Publishing manager: Penny Craig
Publisher: Cindy Richards

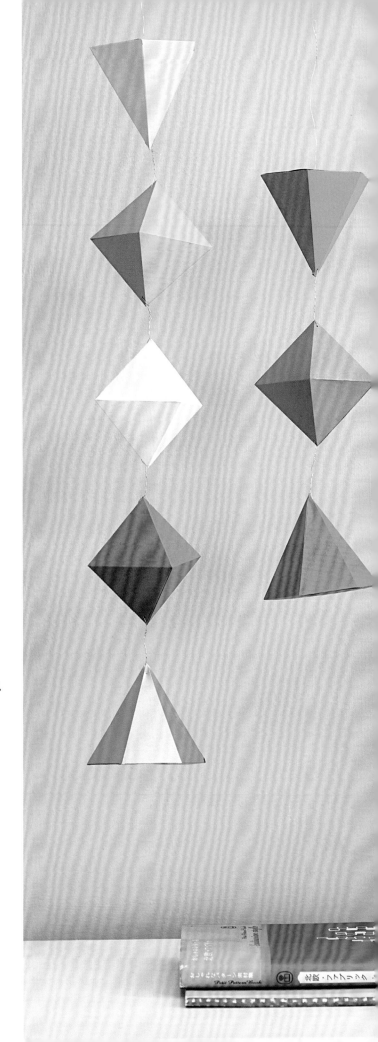

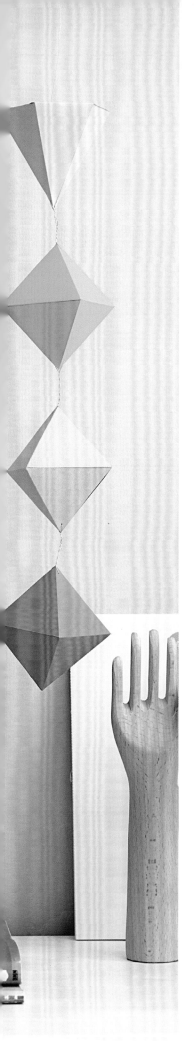

CONTENTS

INTRODUCTION

In the last few years we have all learned the importance of living a more sustainable lifestyle. We are leaning toward a way of life with fewer purchased items and learning how to make do and mend. My love of repurposing and reusing goes back a long way. I was very lucky as a young child to have a grandma who was a brilliant seamstress. She gave me a bag of small fabric scraps and offcuts which I used to make hundreds of outfits for a tiny teddy bear, beginning my love of creating and sewing. Later, when I had my own children, I reused their old baby clothes (the ones that were too worn out to pass on) to make quilts and soft toys for them. The items were bought because I liked the color or pattern, so it was lovely to extend their life, especially as the clothes held special memories that would live on for many more years.

When I got my first apartment I filled it with upcycled, handmade items. I made drapes from embroidered tablecloths that I had found in a thrift store and repurposed an old coat to make pillows. It wasn't only because I was short of money, which I was! No, it was a conscious design choice because I liked the way the fabrics looked, along with the sense of achievement that I gained from making something beautiful for my home without spending a lot of money. My fabric stash still includes clothing that I no longer wear but I know will be used in my creations.

I also keep a stash of paper. I collect ephemera—printed paper items that have a short-term use and are then thrown away such as packaging, old tickets, postcards, leaflets, and anything that catches my eye. As a collage artist they form an important part of my creations and I am always on the lookout for something interesting to use in my work. My love of collecting extends to the natural world. The changing of the seasons from summer to fall is a wonderful time of the year to forage for materials and an opportunity to get the kids out and about. I often bring back pretty-colored leaves and wonderful dried seed pods and grasses to display around the house. The chance to create projects from these foraged pieces of nature has been a joy.

This book also shows you how to use recycled fabric and paper to make beautiful, original projects, from hanging decorations and wall art to decorative and useful projects for the home. For example, you can learn the art of Boro stitching, the Japanese technique of visible mending, to transform a worn-out pair of jeans into a wearable work of art. Whether you make the projects for yourself, your home, or to give as gifts, I hope you enjoy creating them as much as I enjoyed designing them.

CHAPTER 1

FORAGED MATERIALS

MARK-MAKING TOOLS FROM NATURE

YOU WILL NEED

FOR THE MARK-MAKING TOOLS

- Foraged natural materials such as twigs, dried flowers, grasses, and pine needles
- Small secateurs (not essential but useful)
- Thin wire
- Wire cutters
- Paint (I used gouache and ink, but any paints you have would work)
- Plain paper

FOR THE GREETINGS CARDS

- Templates, page 120
- Card stock (card) (not too thick—you want to be able to fold it)
- Ruler
- Knife or similar, for scoring
- Tracing paper
- Pencil
- Scissors
- Glue stick

I am really into making collages, and I use mark-making techniques to print patterns and textures onto paper for my artworks. One of my favorite methods of mark-making is to make tools from things I have gathered, such as twigs, grasses, and pine needles. When you are out foraging for suitable natural materials, collect a variety and spend some time experimenting. As well as using some of your foraged foliage straight away, you can also make tools that you can use again and again. It doesn't take long to build up an exciting collection of papers that you can use to craft these charming collaged birds to display, frame, or make into greetings cards.

1 To make a "brush" tool, gather together a bundle of long pine needles or tough dried grasses. Select a twig that is about the length of a pencil, but it can be thinner. Push the twig down into the center of the bundle by approximately 1¼in (3cm). Wrap some wire around the pine needles to attach them to the twig. Twist the two ends of the wire and wrap the twisted wire around so that the pine needles or grasses are secure. Trim the ends of the pine needles to roughly the same length.

2 If you have collected a few dried
flower heads, try grouping these
together and securing them with some
wire in the same way as in step 1.

3 To make another style of mark-making
tool, cut a rectangular shape out of
a thick or dried leaf and snip the end
to create teeth like a comb.

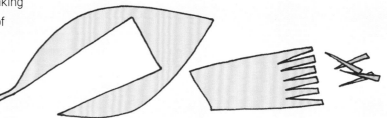

4 A twig cut in half lengthwise will make a semicircle
mark, great for making repeat patterns. Small
secateurs work well for this but you could also
use some small sharp scissors.

5 Use your tools to make some sheets of patterned paper.
Mix up some paint in a small saucer or paint palette.
To make a repeat pattern using a twig (either cut to
a semicircle or cut straight across to make a more
complete circle), dip the end of the twig into the paint
and print a line of marks. Repeat another line under
this one and carry on doing this to make the pattern.
Dip the brush-like tools into the paint. Brush
backward and forward in a sweeping motion to get
some nice textures. You can also dab up and down to make
a stipple effect. Experiment by dipping your tools in the paint
and seeing how many different marks you can make. You can
also let the first layer dry and then make some more marks
on top in another color.

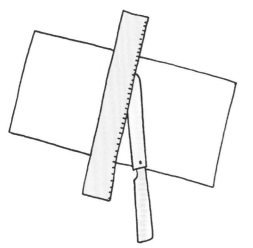

6 To make a collaged greetings card, cut out a rectangle of card stock (card) measuring 12 x 6in (30 x 15cm). Use a ruler and scoring tool such as a cutlery knife to score down the center of the card. Fold the card in half.

7 Trace the templates on page 120 onto tracing paper, and cut out the shapes.

8 Draw around the templates onto your patterned paper and cut out the shapes.

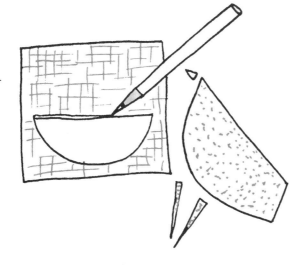

9 Arrange and then stick down the shapes into position on the folded card—see the photo above.

FESTIVE GILDED GARLAND

YOU WILL NEED

- Leaves (you will need approximately 10 leaves per yard/meter of string)
- Sheets of paper or newspaper (for pressing the leaves)
- Some heavy books
- Some strong pieces of paper (copy paper is ideal)
- Paintbrush
- Quick-dry size adhesive (this is the glue that sticks down the gilding flakes. It can be easily obtained from art suppliers)
- Metallic foil gilding flakes
- Soft paintbrush (different than the one you use for the quick-dry size)
- Sponge (not a soft one— a dishwashing sponge with a rough surface on one side is ideal)
- String (I used gold string)

I was very happy with the way the gilding worked on the leaves. With this method, you can turn a few simple green leaves into something truly beautiful. I used metallic foil leaf gilding flakes that had a mix of copper, silver, gold, and pink flakes—they really shimmer and the colors are beautiful. I strung mine together to make a stunning garland, but they would also look wonderful as an embellishment on some gift wrap. You could also stick one down on some folded card stock (card) to make a dazzling greetings card.

1 For this project, the leaves need to be pressed. Place the leaves in between two sheets of paper or newspaper. Place under some heavy books and leave for up to two weeks.

2 When the leaves are completely dried out and pressed, place one of the leaves on a piece of strong paper such as copy paper. Paint the size liquid all over the leaf and stem, making sure you cover everything. Leave the size to dry. Check the instructions on the bottle of size—some take longer to dry than others. I used a quick-dry size, which was ready in approximately 15 minutes.

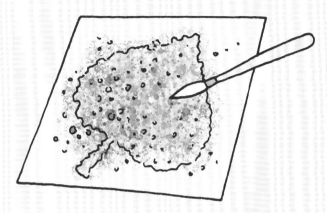

3 Sprinkle the foil flakes all over the leaf and stem, then use a dry soft paintbrush to press the flakes onto the leaf. You can gently press the flakes down with your fingertip, too.

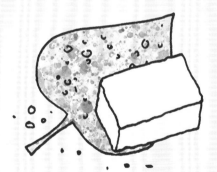

4 Shake off any excess flakes. If there any gaps on the leaves, place a few more flakes in those areas and press them down. Use the sponge to rub over the surface of the leaf. You may think this is going to rub off the flakes, but it doesn't—it burnishes them, so that the surface is smooth and beautifully covered.

5 Repeat steps 2–4 to make a collection of gilded leaves. Tie the stems to some string at equal intervals to make the garland.

GEOMETRIC PEBBLE PAINTING

YOU WILL NEED

- Pebbles
- Masking tape
- Paint in different colors (such as matt emulsion or acrylic paint)

The smoothness of a pebble makes it an ideal surface for painting. I love the simple geometric shapes on these pebbles that make a never-ending display of alternative combinations as you move them around into different positions. Leave areas of pebble unpainted to appreciate the gorgeous natural colors alongside the flat areas of paint. Grouped together they would make a stylish and unusual display in a bathroom.

1 Make sure the pebbles are clean and dry.

2 Decide where you want your first shape to be. For example, you could start by painting one end of a pebble. Position the masking tape around the pebble, making sure it is well stuck down.

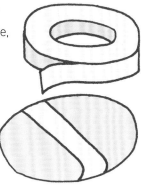

TIP

I used test pots of matt emulsion that I had leftover from doing some decorating, but you could also use acrylic paint.

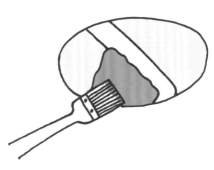

3 Make sure the pebbles are clean and dry. Use a soft brush to paint on your first color. Brush the paint over the edge of the masking tape and onto the area you want to paint, being careful not to get the paint under the edge of the tape. Wait for the paint to dry and then peel off the tape.

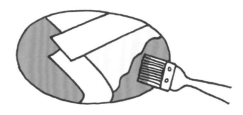

4 Make sure the pebbles are clean and dry. Stick down the tape for the next section. If the next section you want to paint butts up to the first shape, you will need to stick the masking tape along the edge of the painted section. Paint on your next color.

5 Make sure the pebbles are clean and dry. When this section is dry, carefully remove the tape. Sometimes the tape will lift a bit of the paint, but you can easily touch these gaps up with a small paintbrush and paint.

FLORAL HANDMADE PAPER

YOU WILL NEED

- Flowers (you can also use seeds and pieces from dried grasses)—a small bunch will be plenty
- A few sheets of paper (for pressing the flowers)
- Several heavy books
- 2 picture frames in the same size. Mine measured 8¾ x 10¾in (22 x 27cm)
- Net or fly-screen fabric. Mine measured 11 x 12½in (28 x 32cm) for the size of the frames I used
- Scissors
- Staple gun
- Approximately 5–6 sheets of paper (I used copy paper. You can use most scrap papers but avoid glossy paper)
- Large bowl such as a dishwashing bowl or deep tray (it must be bigger than your frames). Mine measured 11 x 15in (28 x 38cm) and was 6in (15cm) deep
- Extra smaller bowl
- Blender (I used a hand-held blender)
- Towel
- Fine cotton fabric—an old pillowslip (pillowcase) is ideal
- Sponge or absorbent kitchen cloth

There is something very special about handmade paper. I have always been drawn to it in art supply shops, and a few years ago I decided to try making my own. It was easier than I thought it would be, great fun, and the equipment needed is mostly household items. Adding seeds and pressed flowers takes the paper to another level of gorgeousness.

1 Remove the flowers from the stems. You can keep some of the small flowers complete and also remove the petals from others to press separately. Press the flowers and petals by sandwiching them between sheets of paper and placing some heavy books on top. Leave them for a couple of weeks.

2 You will need to make a mold and deckle for paper making, which is essentially a screen and a frame. Remove the glass and backing board from your frames, as you won't need those. To make the mold, cut out a rectangle from a piece of net—it needs to stretch over the frame and fold around the edge to the back with enough fabric to staple it to the frame. Use the staple gun to attach the net to the frame. Pull the netting tight as you staple it down. It is best to staple in the middle of each side section and then start pulling tight and working your way around with the staples, until the screen is secure.

TIP

If you use wildflowers, just take a few, don't pull up the roots, and know what you are picking—don't take anything rare. You may be able to find what you need by foraging in your own garden. I found all mine not far from my back door—admittedly quite a few were weeds, but they are pretty too!

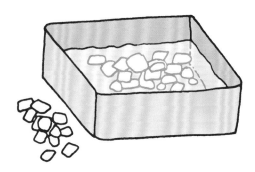

3 Tear up 5 or 6 sheets of paper into small pieces and place them in the large bowl or tray. Cover well with warm water. Leave to soak for a couple of hours.

4 Gather the soaked paper and place it in another bowl. Use the blender to break it down into a fine pulp.

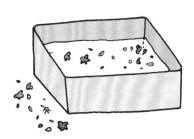

5 Tip out any remaining water from the paper-soaking bowl and fill it with fresh water to a depth of approximately 4–4¾in (10–12cm). Tip the paper pulp into the water and mix for a minute to create a slurry. At this point, mix in the dried flowers and petals. You can experiment with the ratio of pulp to water. The more pulp, the thicker the paper. If the slurry is too thin, it may not cover the screen and the paper may have holes in it. I used approximately 7 pints (4 liters) of water.

6 Place the mold and deckle together, with the unstapled side of the mold facing up and the other frame—the deckle—facing down. Swoosh the slurry around so that the pulp is evenly distributed, and lower the mold and deckle to submerge it in the water. It is best to place it in at an angle then straighten it up under the surface. Move the mold and deckle gently from side to side to get the pulp to lay evenly and then lift the mold and deckle out of the water. If you are not happy with the distribution of flowers, dip it in again and you can help by pushing the petals around a bit. Remove from the water and let the excess water drip though. You could leave the mold and deckle resting on the corner of the bowl for a minute or two.

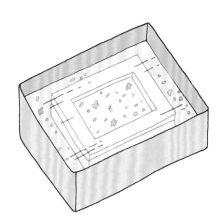

7 Lay a towel down on a flat surface and then place some thin cotton fabric on top. Remove the deckle (the top frame) from the mold. Flip the mold upside down onto the towel and cotton. Press all over the netting with a sponge or absorbent kitchen cloth. Gently lift the mold, leaving the paper on the fabric. Repeat the process—you should be able to make a few sheets from this mix. Leave the sheets to dry on the towel and thin cotton for a day or two. The paper sheets will lift easily from the cotton fabric.

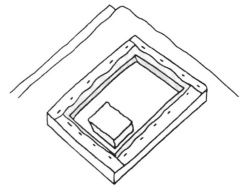

A WALK IN THE WOODS

YOU WILL NEED

- Selection of dried seed pods and leaves
- One twig
- Cotton thread or twine
- Florist's wire
- Wire cutters

Turn a walk in the woods into a foraging expedition to provide materials for this nature-inspired mobile. It's a great project to get the kids involved in—they will love making found treasures into something special. Feathers, small pebbles, and seashells would work well, too.

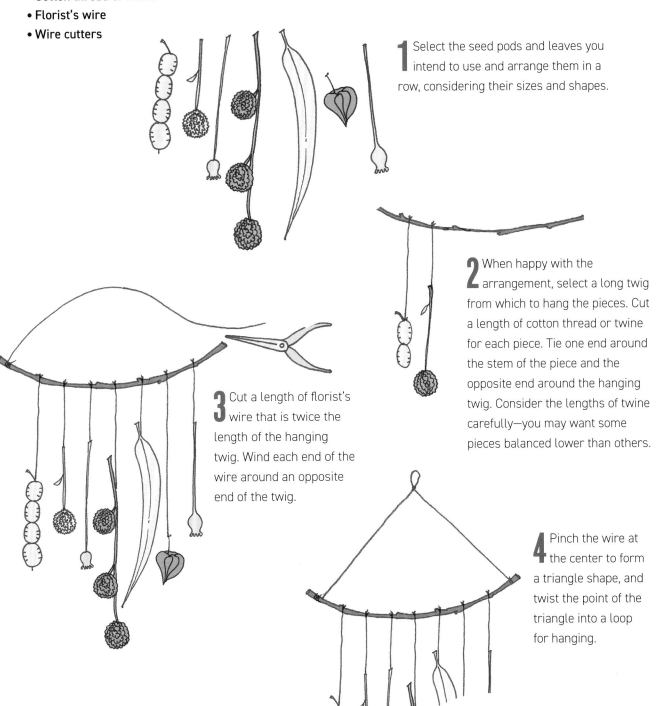

1 Select the seed pods and leaves you intend to use and arrange them in a row, considering their sizes and shapes.

2 When happy with the arrangement, select a long twig from which to hang the pieces. Cut a length of cotton thread or twine for each piece. Tie one end around the stem of the piece and the opposite end around the hanging twig. Consider the lengths of twine carefully—you may want some pieces balanced lower than others.

3 Cut a length of florist's wire that is twice the length of the hanging twig. Wind each end of the wire around an opposite end of the twig.

4 Pinch the wire at the center to form a triangle shape, and twist the point of the triangle into a loop for hanging.

LEAFY WRAP AND GIFT TAGS

YOU WILL NEED

- Selection of leaves and foliage
- Paper (I used a roll of white craft paper and some brown parcel paper)
- Spray paint (I used chalk paint)
- Sticky tack (optional)
- Paint in one or two colors (I used acrylic)
- Paintbrush
- Card stock (card) for the gift tags (I used gray board)
- Ruler
- Pencil
- Craft knife
- Cutting mat
- Hole punch
- String

Giving and receiving gifts is always wonderful but when they are wrapped in handmade paper it becomes something very special. It's simple to make, the results are beautiful, and your friends and family will appreciate all the care you have put into it. Complete the look with some pretty matching gift tags. This would work very well all year round but especially at Christmas—greenery and berries tucked behind the bow would make a lovely festive embellishment. I used two different methods, one using spray and the other with painting onto the leaves and printing; they mix and match perfectly.

1 To make the wrap using spray paint, arrange the foliage on the paper. I used some fern fronds. Spray over the foliage and the whole surface of the paper with the spray paint, making sure you are spraying directly down onto the leaves. If you find the leaves are curling up a bit and the paint is going underneath them, secure them down with a few small pieces of sticky tack. Lift the leaves away from the paper.

2 To make the printed wrap, first select some leaves. Using a paintbrush, paint all over one side of their surfaces, on the leaves and the stalks. I like to paint the back of the leaves as the center rib and veins are more prominent on that side. Position the leaves on the paper, paint side down. Rub all over the leaves to transfer the paint to the paper. You may find it helpful to lay a thin piece of paper over the leaves before rubbing them. Lift up the paper covering the leaves, if using, then lift away the leaves. Repeat this process to build up your design over the whole of the paper. If you would like to create leaf prints in two colors, let the first color dry before creating prints with some more leaves and a second paint color.

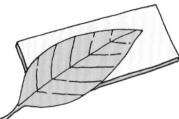

3 To make the tags, use a pencil and ruler to draw some oblong shapes on the card. I made mine 2 x 4¾in (5 x 12cm). Place on a cutting mat and use the ruler and a craft knife to cut out the shapes. Print these in the same way, using either of the methods above.

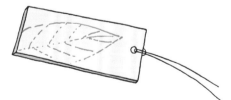

4 Use the hole punch to punch a hole at one end of each tag, making it central and ⅓in (1cm) down from the top edge. Thread some string through the hole to complete the tag.

SEAWEED PRESSING

YOU WILL NEED

- Selection of seaweed
- Bowl (such as a dishwashing bowl or a tray that is bigger than your biggest piece of paper)
- Sheets of watercolor paper (I used some in Letter/A4/42 x 29.7cm and Half-letter/A5/ 29.7 x 21cm sizes)
- Small pair of scissors
- Small soft paintbrush
- Sheets of posterboard (cardboard) (I used packing posterboard from the recycling bin)
- Old towels
- Thin cotton fabric—old pillowslips (pillowcases) are ideal
- Heavy books

I think most of us remember clambering over rocks at the beach, with a bucket in one hand, a little net in the other, and paddling into pools to see what we could discover. For me, staring down into those clear pools of marine life in miniature is a pleasure that has never left me. The strange forms and delicate stems and fronds of seaweed in shades of greens, reds, and browns are fascinating and swaying in the water they look quite beautiful. I have discovered how to capture this by pressing foraged seaweed to create wonderful little works of art. It takes a few days but the wait is worth it and you will be truly amazed at the results.

1 Place your seaweed in a bowl or a sink of water to wash off any sand.

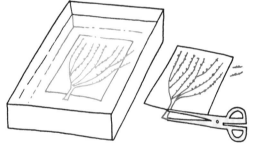

2 Fill the bowl or tray with water to a depth of approximately 2½in (6cm). Select a piece of seaweed to press. Place a sheet of the watercolor paper in the water and the seaweed on top of the paper. Check that the seaweed fits nicely on the paper when it is spread out. You can carefully lift the paper and seaweed out of the water and use the small scissors to trim any of the sections, so that it is a nice shape and fits on the paper.

TIP

Always take seaweed that is unattached to rocks and floating free, or strands that have been washed up on the beach. Just take what you need.

3 Place the paper and seaweed back in the water and gently agitate the water so that the seaweed spreads out nicely over the paper. When you are happy with the position, gently lift the paper. Do this carefully by tilting the paper to one side and letting some water run off it before lifting it completely. This way the seaweed should stay in position.

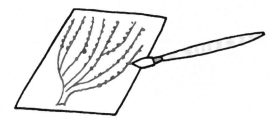

4 Use the paintbrush to gently tease out any delicate fronds. Repeat steps 2–4 to create the number of seaweed pressings you would like to make.

5 Now you can press your sheets of seaweed. Place a piece of posterboard (cardboard) on a flat surface with a towel on top. Lay the sheets of paper and seaweed on top of the towel, followed by the thin cotton fabric, another towel, and then finally another piece of posterboard (cardboard). If you have more sheets of paper and seaweed you can add that on top and repeat the layers. You can make a few layers—I ended up making three.

6 Now cover the layers with a few heavy books. The following day, replace the towels with dry ones. Do this for three days and then leave for a few more days, until the seaweed pressings are completely dried out. You could frame your seaweed pressings or display them on a wall as they are.

PRETTY SEED POD COASTERS

YOU WILL NEED

- Paper, pencil, ruler, set square, and scissors (for making the template)
- Air-dry clay (I used approximagely 1lb 12oz/800g to make a set of 6 coasters)
- Rolling pin
- Wax paper (greaseproof paper) (not essential but useful)
- Something to cut the clay (I used a non-serrated cutlery knife)
- Dried seed pods, flowers, and grasses
- Felt
- Fabric glue
- Matte Mod Podge or similar matte sealant
- Paintbrush

Throughout the year as flowers die back, they leave behind a wonderful array of dried seed pods. With so many variations of shape and form, each one is uniquely beautiful. It is lovely to bring a few in and display them in a vase, but you could take it a step further and capture all their delicate beauty in a set of coasters. I was amazed at how much detail was achieved by pressing the seed heads and grasses into the clay. I also love to use these as pretty plaques to prop up and display on a shelf alongside other foraged natural treasures.

1 On a sheet of paper, use a pencil and ruler to draw out a square to use as a template for your coasters. I made my coasters 4 x 4in (10 x 10cm). Use a set square to draw the corners so that they are right angles. Cut out the template.

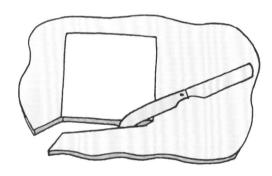

2 Read the instructions on your pack of air-dry clay. It usually says to knead the clay for a few minutes before rolling it out. Use a rolling pin to roll the clay out to a thickness of approximately ¼in (5mm). Air-dry clay can be a bit sticky, so I find it helpful to roll it out on a piece of wax paper (greaseproof paper). Place the template on the clay and use the knife to cut around the edge. Repeat to cut out the number of coasters you would like to make.

3 Use the knife to cut around each corner on the coasters to make them nice and rounded.

4 Select one of your seed heads, dry flowers, or grasses, and press it into the surface of the clay. You can mix it up a bit by using two or three different types of plant on the same coaster, or keep it simple with one type. Lift away the seed head. Don't worry if some seeds are left behind in the clay—you can remove these with a brush when the clay is dry.

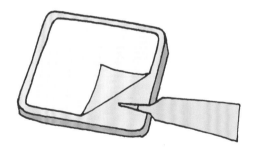

5 Cut out squares of felt that are about ⅛ in (2mm) smaller than the paper template all around. Use fabric glue to stick these down on the underside of the coaster.

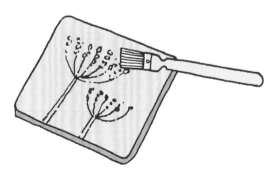

6 Finish by painting a layer of Matte Mod Podge or similar matte sealant over the top surface of the coaster. Leave to dry.

DRIED FLOWER HOLDERS

YOU WILL NEED

- Rolling pin
- Clay or air-dry clay
  (I used approximately
  1lb 5oz/600g for
  a set of 7 holders)
- Wax paper
  (greaseproof paper)
- Ruler
- Knife to cut the clay
  (I used a non-serrated
  cutlery knife)
- Scissors or small
  secateurs
- Something pointed such
  as a wooden skewer
  or knitting needle

Dried seed pods and pretty grasses are abundant in the late summer and fall, and it is easy to gather a bunch of different varieties. You could display them together in a vase, but sometimes it is nice to pick out just a few to show off their individual beauty. I made these little clay holders, decorated with indents made from the twigs and foliage. Each one holds a single grass or dried flower, and placed in a group they make an unusual and charming display.

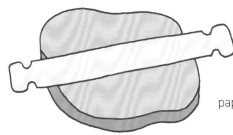

1 Use the rolling pin to roll out some clay to a thickness of approximately ¾in (2cm). Sometimes the clay is a bit sticky, so I find it helpful to roll it on wax paper (greaseproof paper).

2 Use the ruler and knife to cut some small oblong and square shapes from the clay. Mine ranged between 1⅜ x 1⅜in (3.5 x 3.5cm) and 1½ x 2½in (4 x 6cm).

TIP

I used some clay that I happened to have, but you can use air-dry clay which is readily available at craft suppliers. The holders will not get wet, so there's no need to use clay that you would need to fire.

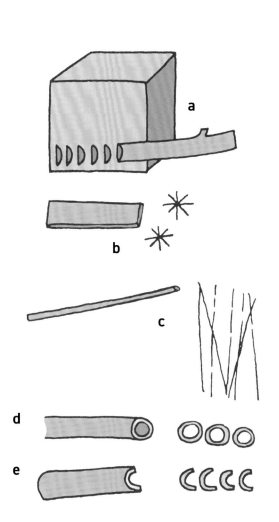

a

b

c

d

e

3 Make some repeat patterns in the clay to decorate them. Experiment with different twigs and foliage on some spare off-cuts of clay, to find shapes that you like. Use the secateurs to cut sticks in half lengthwise to make a tool that prints semicircles (a). I cut a ½in (1cm) strip from a thick dry leaf and pressed it into the clay several times at different angles to make star shapes (b). A thin twig repeatedly pressed into the clay will make an overlapping line texture (c). A hollow stem, such as a stem of bamboo, makes nice circles (d), and if you cut this in half down the length, it will make semicircle shapes (e). You will come up with all sorts of interesting shapes and textures, depending on the foliage you collect. That is all part of the fun!

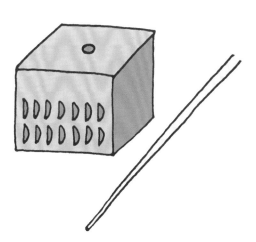

4 Using something sharp such as a wooden skewer, make a hole in each of the tops of the blocks. Press the hole down to nearly the bottom of the block. Leave the blocks to dry.

FRESH FLOWER CHANDELIER

YOU WILL NEED

- Thick wire
- Tape measure
- Wire cutters
- Bullnose pliers
- Thin wire
- 5 small glass bottles
- Fresh flowers

The little bottles that feature in this project are easy to find if you look at online stores for flower arranging and wedding favors. Hung from a wire base and filled with a pretty mix of fresh flowers, they make a truly stunning decoration. Be sure to use thick wire—the bottles hold water and can get heavy.

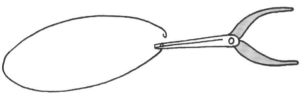

1 Cut a length of thick wire measuring 33in (84cm). Bend the wire to form a ring and use pliers to bend a small loop at one end and a small hook at the other end. Place the hook into the loop, and squeeze together to secure.

2 Cut two lengths of thick wire measuring 1¼in (3cm) more than the diameter of the ring you made in step 1. Use pliers to wrap one end of the first wire around the wire ring—I started at the join.

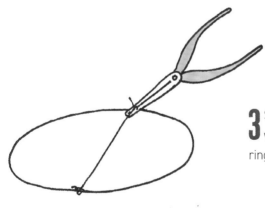

3 Stretch the wire across the ring and wrap the opposite end around the ring. Trim off any extra wire.

4 Rotate the wire ring by 90 degrees and attach the second length of wire in the same way, so that the two wires cross at the center. Where the wires cross at the center, loop the second wire, around the first, to secure.

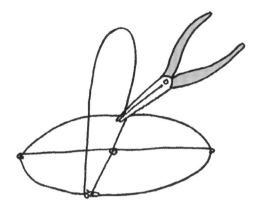

5 Now cut two lengths of thick wire measuring 20in (50cm). Attach the ends to the same points on the wire ring that you attached the wires in steps 2, 3, and 4.

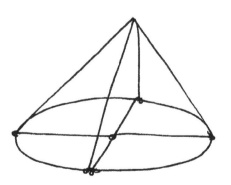

6 Squeeze each wire at the center into a triangle shape.

7 Cut five varying lengths of thin wire that measure between 11 and 13½in (28 and 34cm). Take one length of wire and use pliers to make a small loop at one end. Wrap the looped end of the wire around the top of a bottle, thread the opposite end of the wire through the loop, and pull tight.

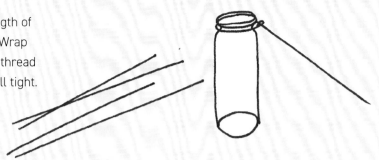

8 Make a small loop at the opposite end of the wire, to hook over the wire ring. Repeat steps 7 and 8 with all the other bottles.

9 Hook four of the bottles over the edge of the wire ring, placing them at those points where the hanging wires have been attached. Place the fifth bottle where the wires cross at the center of the ring.

10 Now for the fun! Pour a small amount of water into each bottle and arrange a pretty mini-bouquet of flowers in each one.

11 You can hang the mobile from a hook screwed into the ceiling.

CHAPTER 2

PAPER AND CARD

CIRCLE GARLAND

YOU WILL NEED

- Scraps of pretty paper
- Coin
- Pencil
- Scissors
- String
- Tape measure
- Craft glue

Choose your prettiest scraps of paper for this sweetest of garlands. I have used some gorgeous Japanese papers mixed in with offcuts from greetings cards and craft papers. The finished garland looks lovely strung on an arrangement of spring twigs.

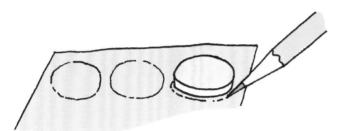

1 Draw around something circular onto the backs of the scraps of paper. I used a coin approximately ¾in (2cm) across.

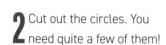
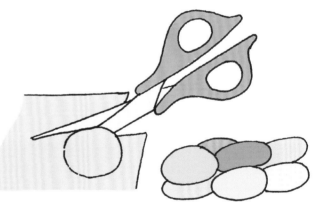

2 Cut out the circles. You need quite a few of them!

3 Cut a length of string. I made my garland approximately 60in (150cm) but you can make it as long as you wish.

4 Pair up the paper disks and stick them, wrong sides together, along the length of the string, sandwiching the string between the disks. Place the disks at regular intervals—I made them approximately ½in (1cm) apart.

FLORAL PAPER BAGS

YOU WILL NEED

- Letter-size (A4) sheets of graph paper and lined paper, two sheets per bag
- Pictures of flowers and pretty labels
- Pencil
- Ruler
- Craft knife
- Cutting mat
- Craft glue
- Pinking shears (optional)

Slip a slice of cake into one of these little paper bags at the end of a summer tea party. Your guest will treasure the bag long after consuming its contents. If you are planning a summer wedding with a vintage feel these would make perfect favor bags. This is a great way of using up sheets of paper in an old exercise book or graph-paper book.

1 Use a photocopier to copy images of flowers and pretty labels onto sheets of graph paper and lined paper. For each bag, cut two rectangles from the paper: one measuring 9½ x 8½in (24 x 22cm) and one measuring 5½ x 8½in (14 x 22cm). Use a craft knife to cut the paper and protect your work surface with a cutting mat.

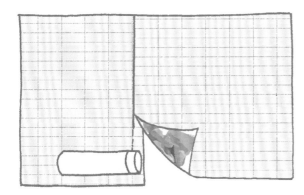

2 Use glue to stick the two rectangles together along one 8½in (22cm) edge, so that they overlap by ½in (1cm). Use a pencil and ruler to measure the overlap if you like. Make sure any images on the two pieces of paper are the same way up.

3 Place the paper, pattern side up, on your work surface with one short edge at the bottom. You are going to make a series of folds to form the bag's front, back, and sides. First, fold the bottom edge up by 1in (2.5cm).

4 Turn the paper over, and repeat step 3, folding what is now the bottom edge up by 1in (2.5cm), (accordion-style). Then fold the new bottom edge up 4¾in (12cm).

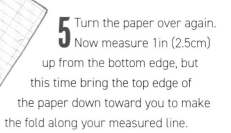

5 Turn the paper over again. Now measure 1in (2.5cm) up from the bottom edge, but this time bring the top edge of the paper down toward you to make the fold along your measured line.

6 Repeat the accordion-style fold in step 4, bringing what is now the bottom edge of the paper up to make a second fold, 1in (2.5cm) up from the bottom.

7 You should be left with a ½in (1cm) overlap at what is now the top edge of the paper. Fold this under, and stick it to the inside of the very first fold you made in step 3. You will have made a paper tube with two pleated sides.

TIP
Leaf through old books and journals for suitable images.

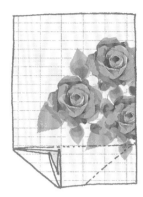

8 Rotate the paper tube so that one short edge is at the bottom and the printed images are the right way up. Fold the bottom edge up by 2in (5cm), crease firmly, and unfold again. Fold each of the two bottom corners in toward the fold you just made, crease firmly, and unfold again.

9 To create the base of the bag, manipulate the creased folds you made in step 8. Open the paper tube slightly and invert the two folded triangles as you do so. They will form the base at each side of the bag. You will be left with two triangular flaps—one at the front of the bag and one at the back.

10 Glue the underside of the front flap, and stick it to the base you made in step 9. Then glue and stick the underside of the back flap in the same way.

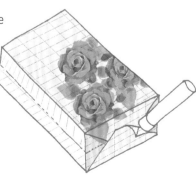

11 Use pinking shears, or similar, to cut a decorative edge across the top of the bag.

POSTAGE STAMP CARDS

YOU WILL NEED

- Selection of suitable images, as squares or rectangles
- White paper
- Pencil
- Craft glue
- Small sharp scissors
- Brown card stock (card), measuring 5½ x 8¼in (14 x 21cm), folded in half
- Block of wood measuring approximately 4 x 2in (10 x 5cm)
- 3 lengths of string measuring approximately 5in (13cm)
- Black ink-stamping pad
- Craft knife
- Cutting mat
- Eraser
- Ruler
- Red and blue ink-stamping pads
- White or pale blue paper

Cut out attractive images from all those old birthday cards you can't bear to throw away or look through magazines and books for suitable pictures. Recycle them to make this unusual card—perfect for a mother's day celebration. For a father's day card, simply pick different images. To complete the postal theme, print some airmail-style gift wrap.

1 Choose three images and glue each to a piece of white paper. They can be different sizes—my largest measured 1½ x 2in (4 x 5cm) and the smallest 1¼ x 1½in (3 x 4cm). Draw a ⅛in (3mm) border all the way around the outside of each image and cut out.

2 Using sharp scissors, cut small semicircular nicks all around the edge of each image to give the appearance of the torn perforations on a stamp.

3 Glue the three images to the front of the brown card stock (card), positioning them in a row in the top half of the card.

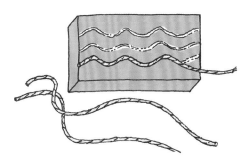

4 Using a pencil, draw three wavy lines across the width of the wood, approximately ½in (1cm) apart. Squeeze glue along each line and position a short length of string over the top. Trim off any spare string at either end of the block.

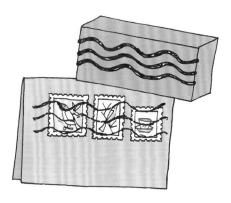

5 Once the glue has dried, press the string down on the black ink-stamping pad and print over the line of images on the brown card stock (card). The ink may print unevenly, but this is the realistic look you want to achieve.

6 Make some airmail gift wrap. Using a craft knife, and protecting your work surface with a cutting mat, cut two small stamps from the eraser, each measuring ½ x ¼in (1 x 0.5cm). Cut the short ends of each stamp on the diagonal.

7 Use the stamps to print airmail lines across the white or blue paper, alternating red and blue ink.

TIN-ROOF HOUSES

YOU WILL NEED

- Brown card stock (card)
- Pencil
- Ruler
- Craft knife
- Cutting mat
- Tracing paper
- Disposable tin cookie sheet (baking tray)
- Tin snips
- Masking tape
- Ballpoint pen
- Craft glue
- Hole punch
- Twine

Transform a disposable tin cookie sheet (baking tray) and some brown card stock (card) into these little decorations. They are so simple to make. Threaded with red and white baker's twine and hung from painted twigs, they make a charming festive display. Use the first one you make as a template and then use the same process to make a whole village of houses, changing the shape and pattern as you like for each one.

1 Protecting your work surface with a cutting mat, use a craft knife to cut a rectangle of brown card stock (card) measuring 4 x 2⅓in (10 x 6cm). Cut out four windows and a door. Don't be too precious about getting the measurements exactly right, any uneven cutting adds to the folksy look!

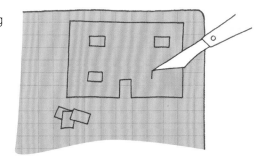

2 Draw out the shape for the roof section on tracing paper, making the roof 1in (2.5cm) wider than the house. Place the tracing on a flat piece of tin cut from the cookie sheet and secure the ends with some masking tape.

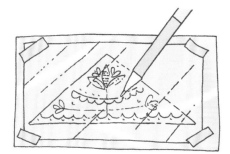

3 Using an old ballpoint pen (it can even be one that has run out of ink), go over the main outline of the roof section. Then use the pen to draw the pattern (use the the photograph opposite as a guide). Press hard with the ballpoint pen to make a good impression in the tin. This is the back of the roof.

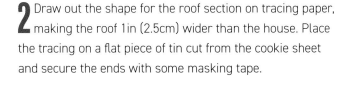

4 Use snips to cut out the tin triangle. Spread glue along the bottom edge and stick it to the top edge of the house.

5 Follow steps 2 and 3 to make the decorative strip that goes across the front of the house, and stick it in place.

6 Punch a small hole at the top of the roof, in the center, and thread through some twine for hanging.

7 Using your first house as a model, cut out more card-stock (card) rectangles, each one a different size. Make some tall and thin, others wide. Cut out windows and doors. Design tin roofs for them, making sure each one is a little wider than the width of its house. Draw different decorations across the roofs: try zigzags, scallops, and dots. Follow steps 4 to 6 to complete each little house.

TIP
Be extremely careful when cutting tin, as it has very sharp edges. It is best not to use your best dressmaker's scissors—use tin snips instead.

PAPER CASCADE

YOU WILL NEED

- 3¹/₈in (8cm) diameter circle template
- Colored paper (wallpaper and recycled gift wrap are fun to use)
- Scissors
- Twine or thick thread
- Craft glue
- Hoop (I used a 8-in/ 20-cm) metal hoop from a craft supplier)

This mobile is so simple to make, yet makes a stunning focal point in a contemporary interior. It looks great hanging in a corner and you can change the lengths of the strands to suit its position. I chose a simple color palette and stayed with it, but you can go wild and use as many colors as you like!

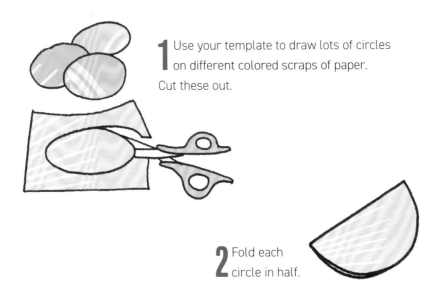

1 Use your template to draw lots of circles on different colored scraps of paper. Cut these out.

2 Fold each circle in half.

3 Take one length of twine measuring 35½in (90cm), glue the back of a circle and stick the two halves together sandwiching the twine between them. Make sure the twine runs along the fold. Have some circles facing one way and some facing the other, for variety.

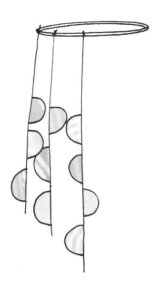

4 Make eight strands of semicircles and tie them to the metal hoop, spacing them evenly around its circumference.

5 Cut four lengths of twine measuring approximately 10in (25cm) and attach to the hoop at the quarter points.

6 Gather the lengths together and tie the ends, making sure that the hoop is horizontal and the mobile hangs straight. Trim off any spare twine before hanging. You can hange the mobile from a hook screwed into the ceiling.

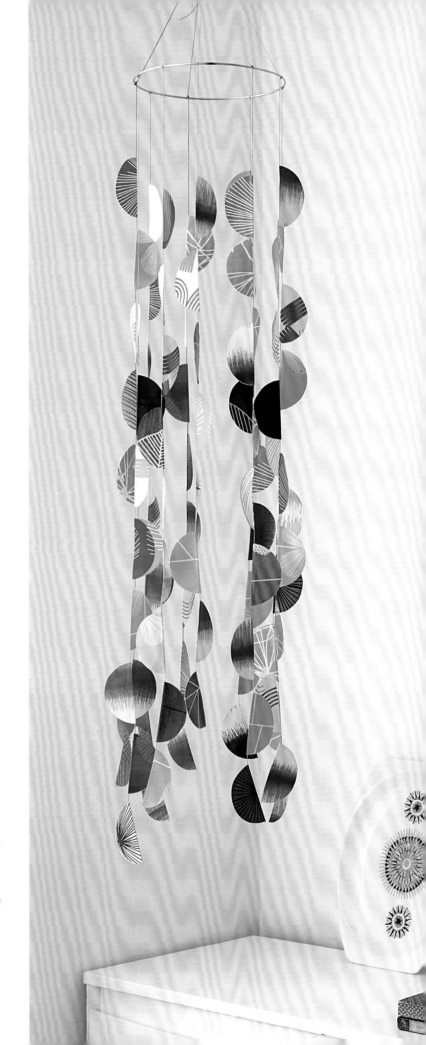

PATCHWORK WALL ART

YOU WILL NEED

- Templates, page 121
- Plain or graph paper
- Tracing paper
- Masking tape
- Pencil
- Thin card stock (card)
- Craft knife
- Cutting mat
- Scraps of paper
- Ruler
- Craft glue

This project couldn't be simpler and looks gorgeous on a bedroom wall. I have used a mix of florals and geometrics in a palette of bright, vibrant colors, using old bits of gift wrap, scraps of wallpaper, and even a section of script typography torn from an old magazine. This is a project that you can easily adapt. Mix geometric patterns with sections cut from old comics, add more typography for a graphic and contemporary look, or mix in sections cut from the kids' paintings and drawings.

1 Enlarge the hexagon templates to the right size using a photocopier. Alternatively, scale them up using graph paper. Trace the templates, transfer them to card stock (card), and cut them out. Use a craft knife and protect your work surface with a cutting mat.

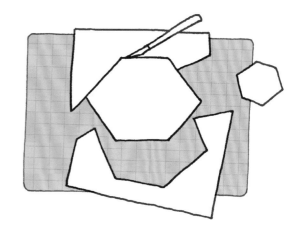

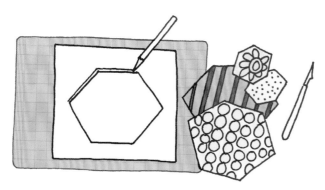

2 Draw around each card template on the backs of different plain and patterned scraps of paper.

3 Cut out your hexagons using a ruler and craft knife for nice crisp edges.

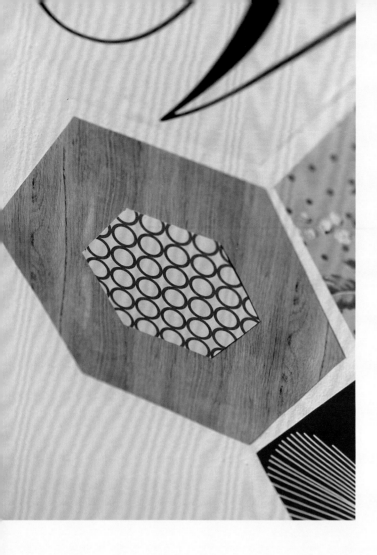

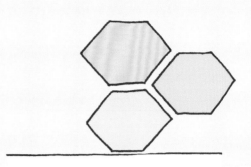

4 Start assembling your patchwork on the wall. Take each large hexagon, spread glue over the back, and position it on the wall. Align the bottom edge of the hexagon with the straight edge of the baseboard (skirting board).

5 Continue until you have stuck down all of your large hexagons, keeping an even gap of ¼in (8mm) between each one.

6 To complete the patchwork, stick some of the smaller hexagons onto the larger ones, centering them by eye. You don't have to put a smaller shape on all of the large ones. It is quite nice to vary it.

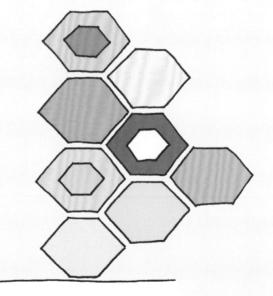

VINTAGE LAMPSHADE

YOU WILL NEED

- Lampshade frame
- Thin paper
- Pencil
- Scissors
- Pages from books
- Masking tape
- Sewing machine
- Washi tape

I found an old frame for a lampshade in a flea market for this design. It was a little rusty, but perfect as a base for a new shade made using a selection of book scraps. You can use anything for this project—old music scores, maps, text, or pictures. I love the mix of black-and-white botanical prints alongside colorful floral pictures from a children's book. It's a real vintage patchwork! If you don't have a sewing machine, you could glue everything together, but I think stitching the paper makes this a very special project.

1 Start by making a pattern for the shade. Take a sheet of thin paper and hold it against one section of the frame. Press down along the edges of that one section, so that you clearly capture the shape.

2 Lay the paper flat and draw along each crease. Now draw an outline ¼in (5mm) outside your original shape. You can do this by placing a number of pencil marks at intervals, each ¼in (5mm) away from the original line, then join them together. Use scissors to cut out the template.

3 My frame has eight panels, so I made up eight panels of patchwork paper. Overlap scraps of book paper to fill each panel, making your shape big enough so that the template fits onto it. Secure with small bits of masking tape.

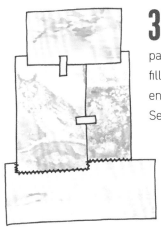

4 Use a sewing machine and zigzag stitch to join the pieces of paper together.

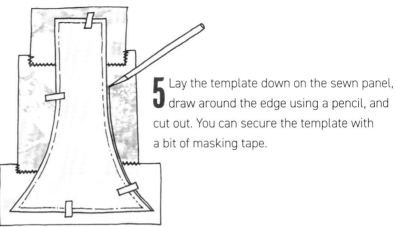

5 Lay the template down on the sewn panel, draw around the edge using a pencil, and cut out. You can secure the template with a bit of masking tape.

6 Repeat steps 3, 4, and 5 to make seven more panels in the same way.

7 Place two of the panels with wrong sides together and use a straight stitch to sew them together, ¼in (5mm) away from the edge.

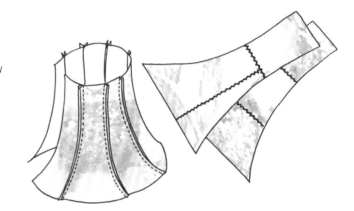

8 Take the next panel and sew this on in the same way. Continue sewing the panels together and stitch the last panel to the first, to complete the circle.

9 Place the shade over the frame. You can secure the paper to the frame using a few small pieces of washi tape. Place on a lamp stand. Mine is made from a recycled bottle that I have decorated using an old bookplate.

TIP

If you are going to make a recycled lamp stand, it is essential that you buy a kit for doing so or get an electrician to do it for you.

GORGEOUS GEOMETRY

YOU WILL NEED

- Tracing paper
- Pencil
- Templates, page 121
- Colored paper or thin card stock (card)
- Masking tape
- Scissors
- Ruler
- Knife or similar, for scoring
- Craft glue
- Needle
- Florist's wire cut into (7in) 18cm lengths
- Small bullnose pliers
- Length of ¼in (6mm) doweling measuring 12in (30cm)
- String or thread, for hanging

For some time now, there has been a huge trend in geometrics in the design, interiors, and fashion world. It is easy to see why. The clean, graphic lines of geometric shapes provide a cool and contemporary look that is adaptable with endless combinations. Use wire and offcuts of colored paper or gift wrap to create this stylish mobile.

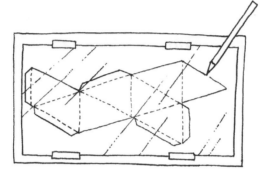

1 Trace out a shape from the templates. Lay the template on the back of a piece of colored paper or card stock (card) and secure with masking tape. Go over the lines using a sharp pencil, making sure to mark the folds with dotted lines, as shown on the template.

2 Cut out the shape. Using the template as a guide, score along the dotted lines using a ruler and the blunt edge of a knife.

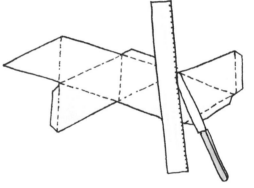

3 Fold all the lines and glue flaps and you will be able to see the shape coming together. Place some glue along the outside edge of the glue flaps and stick them down to the inside of each corresponding edge to form the shape. Repeat this with the other template and make up several shapes in different colors.

4 Use a needle to pierce holes at the top and bottom of one of the shapes. Thread one end of a length of wire though the two holes. Use pliers to bend and twist the wire to secure.

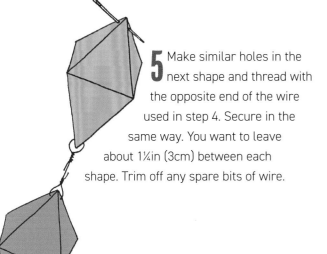

5 Make similar holes in the next shape and thread with the opposite end of the wire used in step 4. Secure in the same way. You want to leave about 1¼in (3cm) between each shape. Trim off any spare bits of wire.

6 To secure a length of wire to a shape with a flat base, fold one end of the wire a couple times to make a T-shape. Make a hole in the center of the flat base. It will need to be slightly bigger than the ones you made in step 4. Gently push the T-shape into the hole—you will need to bend it in line with the wire you are pushing in. Once in, gently jiggle the wire about a bit. It shouldn't come back through the hole.

7 Follow steps 4 to 6 to make three strands of different shapes. When you come to the last shape on each strand, leave the final length of wire long.

8 Wind the top wire of each strand around the piece of doweling, placing one strand at the center and one at each end.

9 Tie a length of thread or string to either end of the doweling, for hanging.

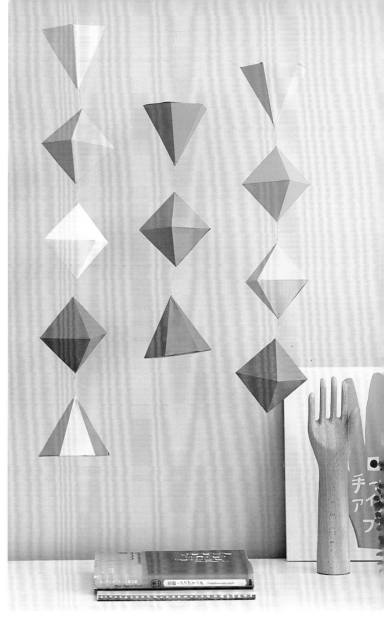

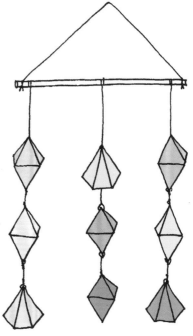

GALLOPING HORSES

YOU WILL NEED

- Templates, page 122
- Plain or graph paper
- Tracing paper
- Pencil
- Masking tape
- Thin card stock (card)
- Craft knife
- Cutting mat
- Craft glue
- Patterned paper (such as recycled gift wrap or wallpaper)
- Awl (bradawl) or similar
- Scissors
- Split pins
- String or waxed cotton thread

These unusual and colorful posterboard (cardboard) horses make a delightful decoration for a child's bedroom wall. Not only do they look fantastic, they have the added wow factor of galloping at the pull of a string! Based on old-fashioned, jumping jack toys, my use of bright, graphic prints gives these horses a contemporary twist.

1 Enlarge the templates for all the body parts of the horse to the right size using a photocopier. Alternatively, scale them up using graph paper. Trace them out and transfer them to card stock (card). Use a craft knife to cut them out, protecting your work surface with a cutting mat.

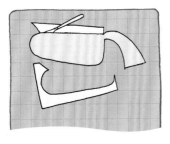

2 Spread glue over the front of the main body of the horse (excluding the tail—you will cover this piece in step 4) and stick it to the wrong side of some patterned paper. Position the shape in such a way that the tail hangs over the edge of the paper, and so won't be covered in paper. Smooth down to stick evenly. Using a craft knife on a cutting mat, cut all around the edge of the body to remove any excess paper. Take care not to cut off the tail.

3 Repeat step 2 to cover and cut out the head and the leg sections of the horse.

4 Now you can cover the tail section. Spread glue on the right side, turn it over, and position it on the wrong side of some patterned paper. This time make sure the horse's body overlaps the edge and so won't be covered. Trim off the excess paper.

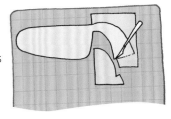

5 Trace out the shapes for the saddle, mane, eye, and head pieces, and transfer them to patterned paper. Cut out each shape and glue in position on the horse.

6 Follow the guides on the templates to make holes in the body and legs. Use an awl (bradawl) or similar.

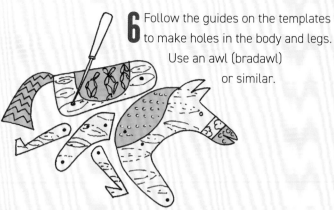

7 Assemble the horse. Start by pushing a pin through the hole in the head section—from the back to the front—and opening the pin to lay flush on the front of the piece. Repeat with the front leg section, pushing the pin through the hole at the top of the leg.

8 Push a pin through the hole at the top of the back leg section in the same way.

9 Use pins to join the lower legs to the upper legs. This time, push the pin through from the front of the horse so that the pin opens up at the back.

10 Follow step 9 to join the head and front leg section together, and the back leg section to the main body in the same way.

11 Cut a length of string or waxed cotton measuring 10in (25cm). Tie each end around one pin at the back of the horse. This joins the head and front leg section to the back leg section.

12 Cut a length of string measuring 12in (30cm). Tie one end around the middle of the loop going from the front to the back legs. Secure it at the middle with a knot and let the rest hang down.

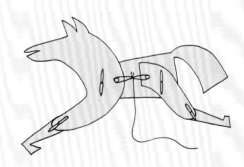

PRETTY PAPER

YOU WILL NEED

- Ruler
- Textured floral paper
- Craft knife
- Cutting mat
- Needle and embroidery floss (thread)
- Length of doweling measuring 21in (54cm)

The success of this mobile lies in getting the balance exactly right. Once you have mastered this, you can make beautiful mobiles using a few basic materials and the minimum of effort. I have used Japanese handmade paper to create a mobile that is charming in a simple and elegant way. You could also use pieces of recycled gift wrap, wallpaper, or the handmade paper from the project on page 20.

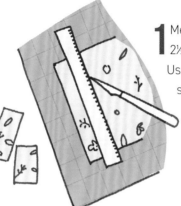

1 Measure several paper strips measuring approximately 2½in (6cm) in width—they can vary by ¾–1in (2–3cm). Use a craft knife to cut them out, protecting your work surface with a cutting mat. Cut the strips into rectangles of varying length between 2¾ and 4½in (7 and 11cm). You need about ten rectangles in total.

2 Use the craft knife to cut out a few shapes on some of the paper rectangles. These will add a pretty element when light shines through the mobile and casts shadows on the wall.

TIP

When cutting the paper rectangles, leave a few of the rough edges that you get with handmade paper, to add a little texture to the mobile.

3 Arrange the paper rectangles into four columns. I placed two lots of three and two lots of two together. Thread a needle with some embroidery floss (thread)—I chose a dark pink color to complement the petals in the paper. Use the needle and floss to join the rectangles together, as shown, tying and cutting the floss to achieve a ½in (1cm) gap between each pair of rectangles.

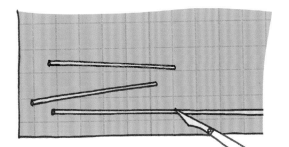

4 Cut three pieces of doweling, each measuring 7in (18cm). You can use a craft knife for this.

5 Use a needle and embroidery floss (thread) to attach a length of floss to the center top of each column of paper rectangles.

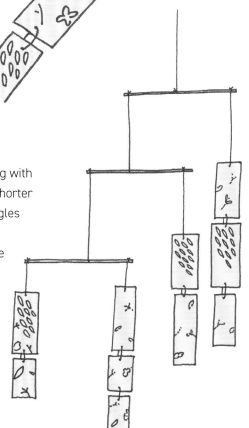

6 Follow the diagram to tie the columns to the doweling, starting with the lower section (note that the lengths of floss (thread) are shorter on this section than on the others). Tie a column of paper rectangles to each end of the doweling. Tie a new length of floss around the center of the doweling and tie the opposite end of the floss to one end of the second section of doweling. Continue in this way to complete the arrangement. Finally, tie a length of floss to the top section of doweling, for hanging. When you hold the mobile up by this last length of floss none of it will balance. You have to slide the floss along the sections of doweling until you achieve the balance.

TIE-CLOSE FOLDERS

YOU WILL NEED

- Adhesive spray
- Patterned paper or wallpaper measuring 12½ x 17¾in (32 x 45cm)
- Thin white card stock (card) measuring 12½ x 17¾in (32 x 45cm)
- Template, page 123
- Tracing paper
- Masking tape
- Pencil
- Ruler
- Craft knife
- Cutting mat
- Knife or similar, for scoring
- Quick-drying strong glue
- 10in (25cm) cotton tape, ⅝in (1.5cm) wide
- Scissors

I am always reluctant to throw away scraps of pretty paper since they come in handy on small craft projects. I also keep postcards, greetings cards, paper bags, candy and fruit wrappers—the list goes on! These little folders are great for keeping everything organized. Make them with smart graphic prints and they will look stunning displayed on your shelves too!

1 Use spray adhesive to glue the patterned paper to one side of the thin card stock (card). Follow the instruction for use on the spray can. Smooth the paper down to make sure there are no creases.

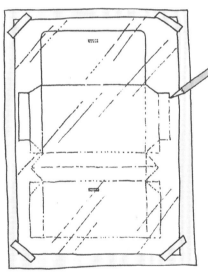

2 Enlarge the template, trace it out, and place it on the white card. Use some masking tape to keep the trace secure and go over all the lines with a sharp pencil.

3 Protecting your work surface with a cutting mat, use a craft knife to cut out the shape, including the two slots for the tape.

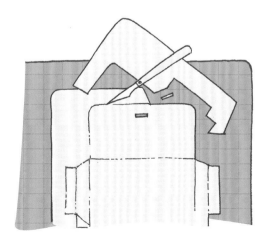

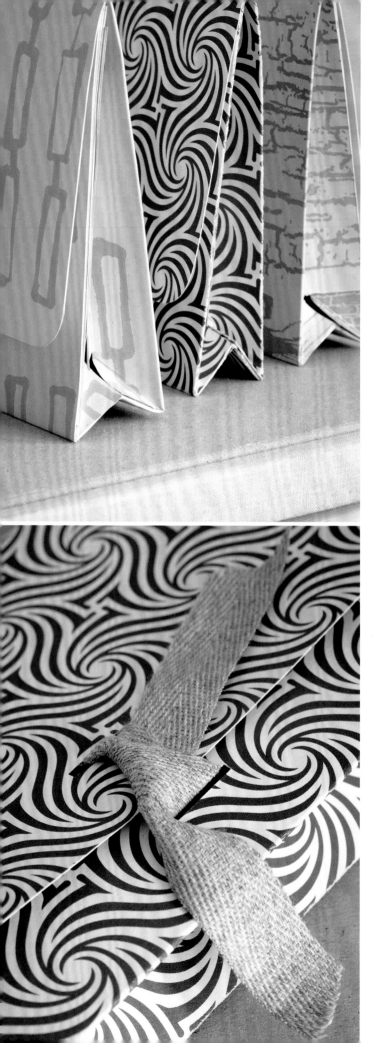

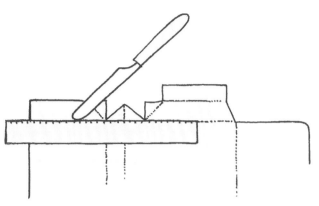

4 Score the lines marked on the template using the blunt edge of a knife or similar.

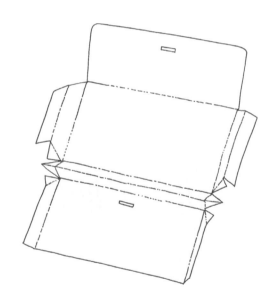

5 Place the shape, white side up, on a flat surface. Follow the guides on the template to fold the card using mountain or valley folds. A mountain fold means you fold toward the back and a valley fold toward the front.

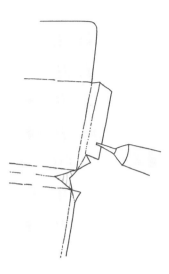

6 Take care when folding the triangle at each end of the base of the folder. Working at one end of the folder first, place some quick-drying strong glue on the two smaller triangles either side of the base and along the side flap of the back section.

7 Bring the front and back sections of the folder together. As you do so, align the two small triangles over the top of the folded single triangle and align the glued side flap with the flap of the front section. Squeeze together gently until the glue has dried a little. Repeat at the opposite end of the folder.

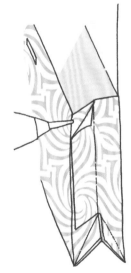

8 Cut two lengths of tape approximately 5in (13cm) long. Thread one end of each length through a slot in the folder. Pull the tape through approximately ¾in (2cm) and glue down. Cut two circles of white paper and stick one over each glued end of tape. Tie the tape to close the flap.

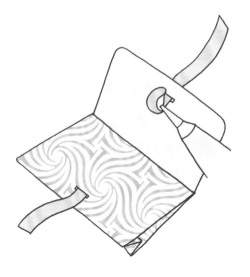

WIRE AND PAPER LETTER

YOU WILL NEED

- Wire
- Tape measure
- Wire cutters
- Masking tape
- Cutting mat
- Craft knife
- Ruler
- Patterned paper
- Craft glue

This unusual and delicate letter is made simply by bending some wire into a letter "O" shape and decorating it with strips of paper. I use all sorts of things, from newspaper and magazine pages, to bits of handprinted paper and gift wrap, old labels, and wrappers. You can use anything you like. Really mix it up!

1 To make the "O" cut two lengths of wire, one measuring 47in (120cm) and the other 32¼in (82cm). Take the longer length and bend it round into a circle, overlapping the ends by about 2in (5cm). Wind a few small pieces of masking tape around the overlap to secure.

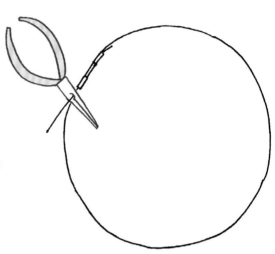

2 Bend the second length of wire into a long sausage shape with straight sides and rounded ends. It needs to fit within the outer circle so that the rounded ends touch it top and bottom. Secure the overlap using small pieces of masking tape.

TIP

When shaping the inner section, make sure the overlap is positioned along one of the straight sides so that it is easier to hide the masking tape under paper.

3 Secure the inner section to the outer section at the top and bottom, using masking tape. When doing this, position the overlapped section of the outer circle to one of the sides so that you can hide it under some paper strips.

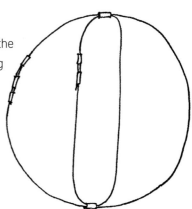

4 Protecting your work surface with a cutting mat, cut strips of paper of varying lengths (mine were between 3½ and 6½in/9 and 16cm). The end result will be more interesting if you vary the widths, too.

5 Working with the letter shape face down on your surface, thread a strip of paper behind the inner and outer sections of wire on one side of the letter. Dot glue on each end and fold these over the wire, sticking them to the back of the paper strip.

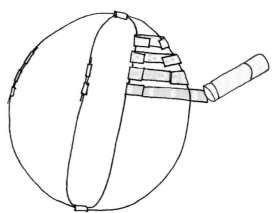

6 To keep it all looking neat, trim off any little corners or edges that do not align properly. Often the back of the letter is just as interesting as the front. I like to leave some gaps so that you can see that the letter is made from wire.

7 Once you have completed your design, either remove the small bits of masking tape holding the two wire sections together, or stick a piece of patterned paper over each of them.

LITTLE WOODEN HOUSES

YOU WILL NEED

- Offcuts of wood cut into different-sized blocks
- White paint
- Paintbrush
- Patterned paper (such as recycled wallpaper or gift wrap)
- Thin white card stock (card)
- Craft glue
- Ruler
- Pencil
- Craft knife
- Cutting mat
- Scraps of lined or graph paper
- Scissors
- Tracing paper
- String

Sometimes the simplest things are the best, like this row of little houses made from a few offcuts of wood and some card stock (card). A tiny garland of puffy clouds completes the charming scene.

1 Paint the offcuts of wood with some white paint. I used acrylic. You may need to apply two or three coats to cover the wood.

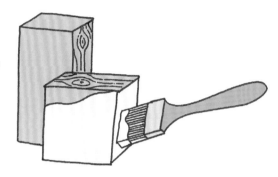

2 Glue a sheet of patterned paper to a sheet of thin white card stock (card).

3 Measure the width of a wooden block and use this measurement to draw a rectangle on the back of the card stock (card) for a roof. The rectangle needs to be twice the depth of the roof you would like and the width of your block. For example, if your block of wood is 2¾in (7cm) wide and you want your roof to be 2½in (6cm) in height, make the rectangle 2¾ x 5in (7 x 12cm).

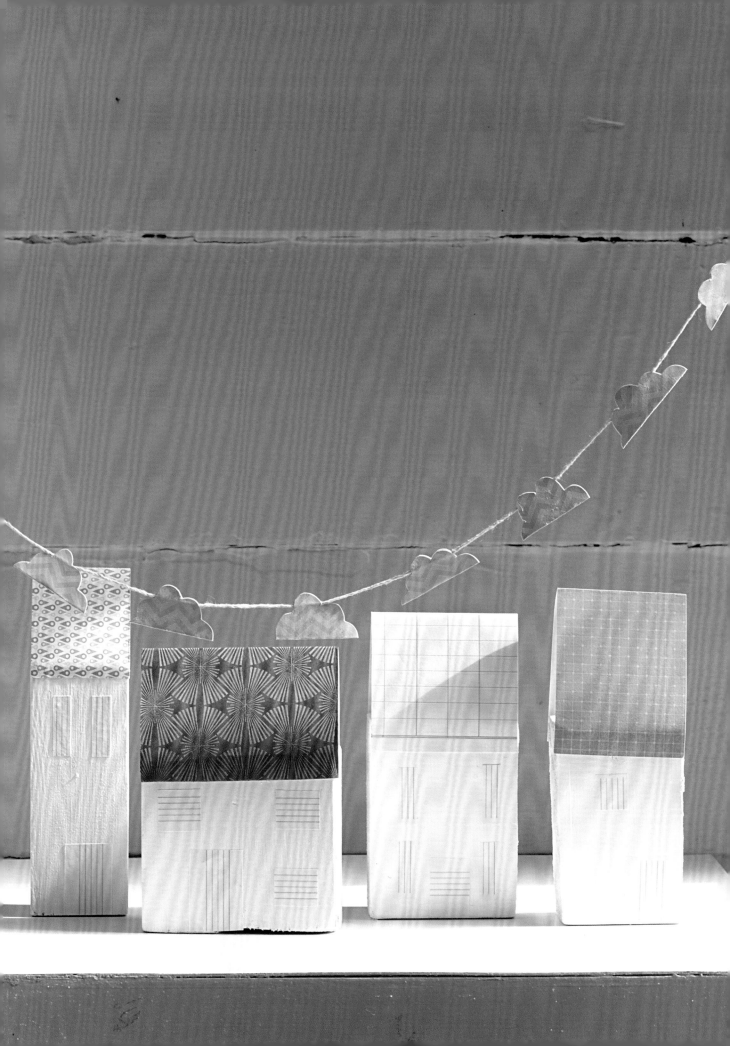

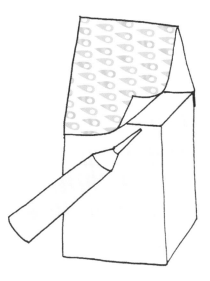

4 Protecting your work surface with a cutting mat and using a craft knife, cut out the rectangle and fold the card stock (card) in half. Run some glue along the top of the wooden block, on either side, and stick the roof to the house.

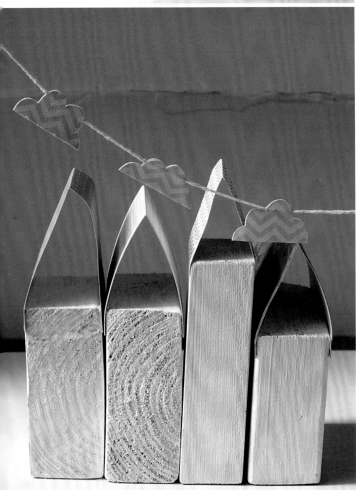

5 Cut out little squares and rectangles of paper to make a door and windows for the house. I used a scrap of paper taken from a music book. Graph paper would work well too.

6 Follow steps 1 to 5 to make several houses with different patterned roofs. Vary the heights of the roofs, too.

7 To make the cloud garland, draw cloud shapes (use the illustration to the right as a guide) onto the back of some patterned paper. Cut out a number of shapes.

8 Fold the cloud shapes in half. Glue the inside surfaces and refold the clouds along a length of string as shown. Leave a little gap between each cloud and try to place the string near the top of each cloud so that it will hang nicely.

TASSELS AND BEADS

YOU WILL NEED

- Scraps of patterned paper
- Pencil
- Ruler
- Scissors
- Craft glue
- Awl (bradawl) or similar, for making holes
- Wire
- Wire cutters
- Bullnose pliers
- Beads in different sizes and shapes
- Nylon thread
- Metal ring measuring ¼in (7mm) in diameter
- Masking tape

Look out for strings of beads in thrift stores and at yard sales. They can cost next to nothing and, combined with some pretty paper tassels and mini fans, can make an eye-catching and original hanging decoration.

1 To make a paper tassel, cut a strip of paper measuring 7½ x 1¼in (19 x 3cm). Cut snips into the long edge—all the way along and ⅛in (3mm) apart. Stop ½in (1cm) short of the top edge.

2 Run some glue along the uncut edge of the strip and roll the paper tightly. Make about 15 tassels this size and one tassel from a strip of paper measuring 7½ x 4in (19 x 10cm).

3 To make a fan, cut a strip of paper measuring 51 x 1¼in (130 x 3cm). Fold back and forth along the strip, making concertina folds approximately ¼in (5mm) apart. Trim off any spare paper at the end. Open up the strip and run some glue along the top inside edge. Fold it up again and squeeze at the top to secure. Make about 15 fans in this way.

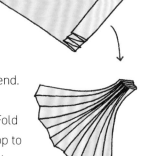

4 Use the awl (bradawl) to make a hole right through the top section of each fan and tassel, positioning it approximately ³⁄₁₆in (4mm) down from the top.

5 To make the larger of the two beaded hoops in this mobile, cut a length of wire measuring 14½in (37cm) and use pliers to make a small loop at one end.

6 Thread a tassel onto the length of wire, pushing it down to the loop at the end. Now thread on some beads and a paper fan. Make sure that the patterned side of the fan faces outward. Continue threading beads, tassels, and fans onto the wire, with ¾in (2cm) of beads between any two paper decorations.

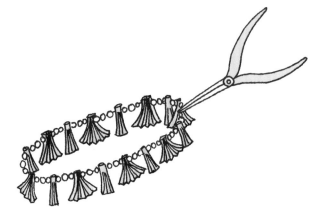

7 Finish off with beads and leave enough wire to make a small loop in the end. Bend the wire around to form a hoop and hook the two looped ends together. Squeeze the join using pliers, to secure.

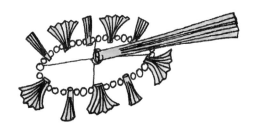

8 Repeat steps 5, 6, and 7 to make the smaller hoop using wire measuring 12in (30cm). Tie a length of nylon thread across the diameter of the hoop and secure with a knot at each end. Tie a second length of nylon across the hoop, but running in the opposite direction so that the two threads cross at the center, as shown. Thread the large tassel onto some nylon and hang this from the center of the hoop.

9 Cut four lengths of nylon measuring 14in (35cm). Tie them to the bottom of the small metal ring and thread all four through beads for about 3in (8cm). Use big beads if you can find them.

10 Now thread each of the four lengths of nylon with beads, using the same number of beads for each strand. Approximately 9½in (24cm) from the end, secure each length with a piece of masking tape, just while you complete all four.

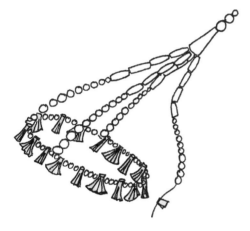

11 Remove the masking tape from each length in turn and tie to the larger beaded hoop, at quarter intervals around the circumference. Cut off any spare wire.

12 Repeat steps 10 and 11 to make four shorter strands of beads measuring 4in (10cm), with extra at each end for tying, and attach each one to the larger beaded hoop at one end and the small beaded hoop at the other.

13 Attach a length of nylon thread to the top of the metal ring, for hanging.

CHAPTER 3

FABRIC AND THREAD

APPLIQUÉ WALL HANGING

YOU WILL NEED

- Letter template
- Plain or graph paper
- Ruler
- Pencil
- Tracing paper
- Masking tape
- Scissors
- Fabric measuring approximately 17½ x 17½in (44 x 44cm)
- Pins
- Air-erasable pen
- Scraps of fabric and paper
- Sewing machine
- Ribbons, buttons, and charms
- Fabric tape
- Needle and sewing thread
- Thin wooden dowel measuring 17½in (44cm) in length
- String

I have a collection of pretty scraps of fabric, embroidered napkins, bits of lace, and trimmings that come in handy for projects like this. For this attractive wall hanging, I have combined paper and fabric, but if you wanted to make yours into a pillow cover, use only fabric, buttons, and trimmings—materials that can be washed in a machine.

1 Choose your letter, or use the template on page 122, and enlarge it to the right size, either by using a photocopier or by scaling the letter up on graph paper. I chose a chunky typeface and made the letter approximately 14in (35cm) in height. Transfer the letter onto some tracing paper.

2 Use scissors to cut the letter out. Pin the letter to the piece of fabric and draw around it with the air-erasable pen or similar.

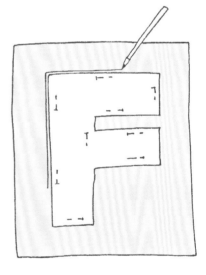

3 Use your pretty fabric and paper scraps to cover the letter shape, pinning them in place once you have an arrangement you like.

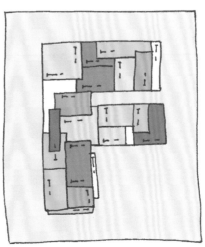

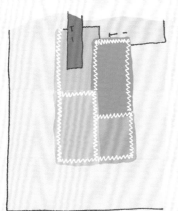

4 Use zigzag stitch on a sewing machine to secure each scrap in place.

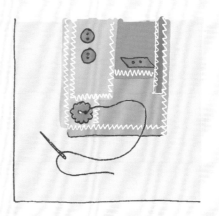

5 Embellish the appliqué letter with lengths of ribbon, buttons, and charms.

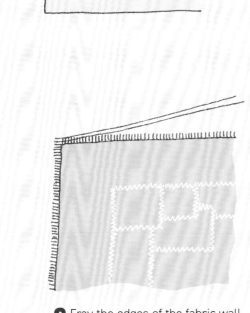

6 Fray the edges of the fabric wall hanging all the way around. You can do this by pulling away the threads that make up the fabric—up to approximately ⅓in (8mm).

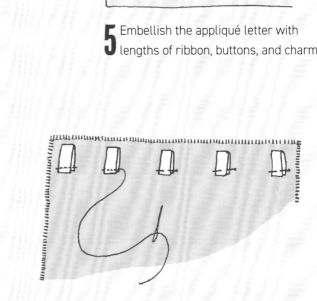

7 Cut five pieces of fabric tape, each measuring 2in (5cm) in length. Fold each in half vertically to make a loop. Pin to the back of the fabric, spaced evenly across its width and with the raw ends approximately 1½in (4cm) down from the top. Using small stitches, sew the raw ends of the loops to the fabric. Take care not to go all the way through the fabric, to prevent the stitches showing on the front of the wall hanging.

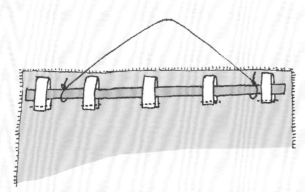

8 Thread the wooden dowel through the loops and tie a length of string to each end of the rod, to use for hanging.

COVERED BUTTONS

YOU WILL NEED

- Motifs and stitch guides on page 123
- Buttons measuring approximately 1¼in (3cm) in diameter with central shank
- Scraps of denim or other fabric, at least 2 x 2in (5 x 5cm) for each button
- Dressmaker's carbon paper
- Red and white stranded embroidery floss (thread)
- Needle and matching sewing thread

These gorgeous buttons are made using traditional motifs and have been stitched onto denim in striking red and white. They would make a lovely gift presented in a little box and could be used on anything from clothes or pillows to quilts or bags.

1 To cover a button measuring 1¼in (3cm) in diameter, cut out some circles of fabric measuring 2in (5cm) in diameter.

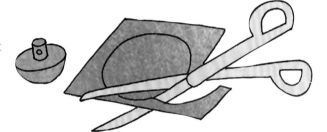

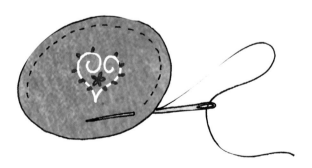

2 Using dressmaker's carbon paper, transfer a motif from page 123 onto the fabric, positioning the pattern in the center of the circle. Embroider the design following the stitch guide.

3 Thread a sewing needle with thread and sew a row of small running stitches all around the circle, ¼in (5mm) in from the edge.

4 Place the circle over the front of the button and pull on the end of the thread to gather the material together. Secure the fabric in place by hand sewing from one side to the other, pulling the gathered fabric tight until the fabric is smooth.

PIN DOLLS

YOU WILL NEED

- Templates and stitch guide on page 122
- Thin wire
- Small pair of pliers
- Scraps of felt
- Needle and matching sewing thread
- Orange and pink stranded embroidery floss (thread) and small amounts of other colors
- Small lengths of ribbon and trimmings

These two enchanting little ladies are based on traditional Guatemalan worry dolls. In folklore, children were told to whisper their worries to tiny pin dolls, place them under their pillow, and the dolls would take their worries away while they slept.

1 Cut three lengths of wire measuring 3½in (9cm). Take the first piece and form it into a loop, twisting the two ends together to secure. Squeeze the loop to make a thinner, elongated shape and twist the loop at about 2in (5cm) down from the top to form the head.

2 Take the second piece of wire and form it into a loop, as in step 1. Squeeze the loop together, fold it in half to find the center, and wrap it once or twice around the neck to form the arms. Repeat for the legs but place the folded piece of wire through the bottom of the body loop. Twist around once to secure and bend the bottom of the wire up a fraction on each end to make the feet.

3 Trace the template on page 112 and cut out a piece of felt for the head. On one side sew a tiny dot for each eye, two tiny dots side by side for the mouth, and a small cross stitch for each cheek. As the stitches are so small you will need to use normal, thin sewing thread. Fold the felt in half and position it over the wire head. Sew up the side seams using small stitches.

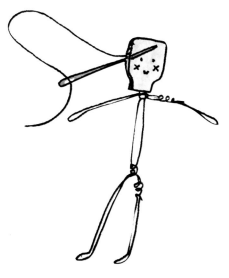

4 To cover the arms, take a length of pink stranded embroidery floss (thread) and wind it around the arm, starting at the hand on one side. Lay the end of the thread along the length of the arm to hide it behind the winding thread.

5 Twist the thread around the neck a couple of times and continue down the arm to the hand, come back up the arm, then continue down the body. You can continue down the legs in the same color or change to another color—I used orange. Come back up the legs to tie off at the body section. It is quite tricky to cover up the wire at the tip of the toes. I tied a tiny amount of thread through the wire, tied a knot, and trimmed it. This hides the wire and adds a tiny tassel for a shoe!

6 Use a 2in (5cm) length of embroidery floss (thread) to make a braid (plait). Use a contrasting color to tie off the braid at each end, and secure it to the back of the head with a few stitches so that the doll has bunches.

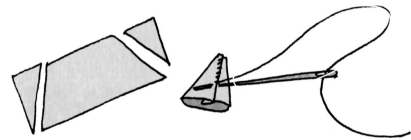

7 Cut a piece of ½in (1cm) wide trimming or ribbon to approximately 1¼in (3cm) long. Cut off two triangles at the corners, one from each side, so that the ribbon is a trapezoid shape. Fold it around to form a cone, tuck under the raw edge with a very small hem and sew together. Place it over the head to make a hat and secure with a few stitches.

8 Trace the template on page 122 and cut out the doll's top from felt or fabric. Embroider a few stitches on the front to decorate. Fold it in half and sew up the side seams. Place the top onto the doll and secure the back with a couple of stitches in a contrasting color.

9 Cut a piece of ⅝in (1.5cm) wide ribbon to approximately 2¾in (7cm) long for the skirt. With right sides together, fold it in half and sew a seam about ¼in (5mm) in from the edge. Turn right sides out and sew a line of running stitch across the top edge of the tube.

10 Place the skirt onto the doll, drawing the line of stitching in tight and placing a few stitches to secure it to the body, under the doll's top. Repeat this with a slightly longer piece of ribbon measuring 3 x 1¼in (8 x 3cm), placing it under the first skirt and reaching down to the feet, to give you a two-tiered skirt.

INDIGO WOVEN MAT

YOU WILL NEED

- A wooden loom
- Twine (I used natural jute)
- Strips of fabric
- Scissors
- Large blunt darning needle with an eye that will take a strip of fabric
- Needle and matching sewing thread
- Pins

I find looking through my vintage craft books a wonderful mindful activity. Those produced in the seventies include lots of colorful weavings—a craft that has gained popularity again, with textile artists producing beautiful and tactile pieces. You need a small wooden loom and some yarn, but you can also create wonderful and unusual pieces using offcuts of fabric. I noticed the lovely frayed selvage edge on some indigo dyed fabric in my stash recently. I thought it was too good to hide away under a hem, so have designed a mat showcasing those edges, made from longs strips of the cloth. The finished result has a lovely textural quality and there was real sensory pleasure in making it. You could use recycled denim for a more robust finish.

1 Prepare the loom with the warp threads—these are the threads that are held in tension across the loom. Tie one end of the twine around the side of the loom at the top. Slip the twine into the first notch and take it down to the corresponding notch at the bottom. Go into this notch, along to the next one and then up again to the corresponding notch at the top. Repeat along the entire width of the loom. Tie off the twine to the side of the loom, making sure that the tension is tight.

2 Cut some selvage from the fabric in long strips approximately ½in (1cm) wide (don't worry too much about exact measurements). Fray the strips back a fraction of an inch. You may not have enough selvage edge to complete the weaving. If this is the case, cut some strips from the main piece of fabric and fray each side of the strip by a fraction of an inch.

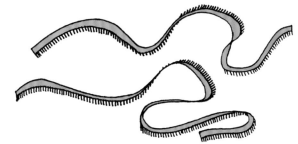

3 Now you can create the weft—the threads that are woven under and over the warp thread. Thread the needle with a strip of fabric. Starting from either side of the loom, weave the fabric strip under the first warp and over the next, leaving a bit of extra fabric at the beginning to finish off later. Carry on across the width of the loom until you reach the end warp thread.

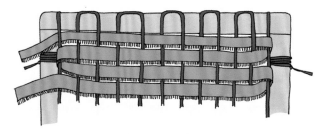

4 Now loop the strip of fabric back over the same warp thread and weave back along the next row. Make sure that the strip is woven in the opposite way to the one above, so if the one above goes over the warp thread, the one on the next row should go under it. Carry on in this way, taking care not to pull too tightly at the edges as this will give the weaving an inward curve. (A loom with a metal bar at each edge avoids this problem.) When you reach the end of each strip of fabric, leave a small length at the edge to finish off later. It is always better to finish a strip at the edge to create a neat finish.

5 When you have filled the loom with weaving, untie the thread you tied to the side of the loom and lift the top and bottom sections to remove the weave from the loom. Thread the side thread onto the needle and finish it off with a few stitches at the back of the weaving, leaving a loop of similar size to the others. Repeat this at the other end.

6 Ease the strips of fabric into position, so they sit evenly on the warp thread. Tuck the loose ends of fabric at the edges through to the back of the weaving and finish off with a few stitches.

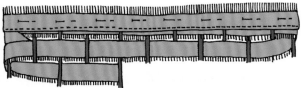

7 You can either leave the mat like this or finish it off with a frayed edge. Cut two ¾in (2cm) strips from the selvage edge of the fabric that are slightly longer than twice the width of the weaving. Turn under a ¼in (5mm) hem. Pin one strip to the top of the weaving, continuing it around the back and overlapping the two ends where they meet. You can use a sewing machine to attach this strip or hand stitch it to secure. Repeat at the other edge of the mat.

BORO-STITCHED JEANS

YOU WILL NEED

- An item of clothing
- Small scraps of fabric
- Scissors
- Pins
- Needle
- Six-stranded embroidery floss (thread)
- Dressmaker's chalk pencil (optional)

Boro stitching is an ancient Japanese technique of visible mending. Patches of fabric and multiple rows of small stitches are used to turn something that may have been worn out and full of holes into an original item of clothing. If you were patching a child's pair of jeans you could use scraps of fabric from clothes that they have long grown out of. As time goes on you can keep adding sections. Recycling in this way means that cherished memories of times gone by are captured and you have created something that is truly beautiful and original. To me that is meaningful and happy stitching.

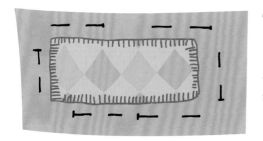

1 To sew a patch where the fabric is placed behind the rip, cut a piece of fabric from your scraps that is ½in (1cm) larger all around than the hole or rip you are patching up. Place it behind the rip with the right side showing through the rip. Pin in place.

2 Thread a needle with two strands of embroidery floss (thread). Decide where you want to position your rectangle of stitches. You can stitch these rectangles of stitches by eye, or you can draw them out with a dressmaker's chalk pencil. Sew a line of running stitch down one side of your planned rectangle, making sure that you go over a section of the scrap fabric. When you sew the running stitch try to keep the space in between each stitch the same length as the actual stitch.

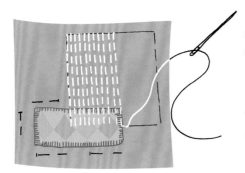

3 Sew another line of stitching next to the first, spacing this line about ⅛in (4mm) away. Continue in this way until you have created a rectangle of running stitches.

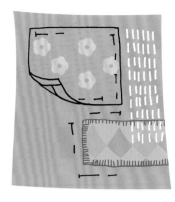

4 To sew a section with a patch on the outside of the garment, cut a rectangle of fabric to the size you want. Turn in a small hem all around and press with an iron. Place the patch in position on the garment and pin in place. Repeat step 2 to create another rectangle of running stitch lines.

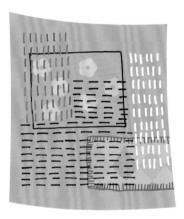

5 Continue making rectangles of stitches overlapping the patches of fabric, varying the direction of the stitching and changing the color of the thread if you like.

6 To make the cross-stitched sections, make the rows of running stitch as before, but space the lines about ¼in (5mm) apart. Then make rows of stitching at right angles to the first rows, crossing over all the stitches in the first row.

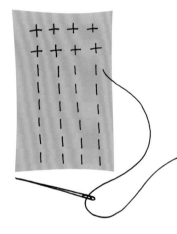

TIP

Mending and patching means your clothes will last longer. It's much more eco-friendly, plus they will look completely unique.

LEAPING TIGER WALL ART

YOU WILL NEED

- Templates, page 124
- Paper and pencil
- Scissors
- Scraps of fabric in different colors
- A sheet of fusible bonding web (such as Wonderweb), measuring about 20 x 20in (50 x 50cm)
- Iron
- Canvas or thick cotton, measuring 19 x 13in (48 x 34cm)
- Two bulldog clips to hang the wall art

You can use small scraps of leftover fabric to create this joyful artwork, which is so easy to make. I've given you a template to follow as a guide, but really you can fill in the spaces exactly how you want, cutting out different stripes and deciding where the lines of stitching go. I used mostly a selection of plain fabrics, but why not bring some patterns into the mix? Really anything goes with this kind of appliqué work—even florals! It is all about having fun.

1 Using the templates on page 124, transfer the shapes for the head, body, and legs onto paper. Cut these out so that you can use them to draw around.

2 Take a piece of fabric that you want to use as the base for the head and body of the tiger. Follow the instructions on your fusible web to iron it onto the wrong side of the piece of fabric you have chosen. Don't remove the backing paper yet. Do the same for the fabric you are using for the legs.

3 Use the templates to draw around and cut out the head, body, and legs.

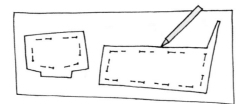

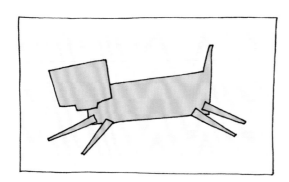

4 Lay them down in position on the canvas fabric, making sure that the tiger is centered on the canvas, with an even border all around. Once you are happy with the position, peel off the backing paper and follow the instructions on the fusible web to iron down and secure.

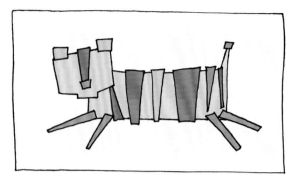

5 Iron some fusible bonding web onto the scraps of fabric you are using for the stripes and details on the face. Leave the whiskers for the moment. Cut out some shapes and start laying them down on the base tiger. You can keep moving them around until you are happy with the composition. I like the stripes to extend beyond the edges of the base shape as it makes a livelier image. When you are happy, peel off the backing paper and iron these down.

6 To make the whiskers, cut two shapes and fray the fabric on one edge. Iron some fusible bonding web onto these pieces, making sure you don't attach any fusible web to the frayed section.

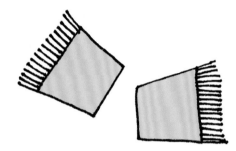

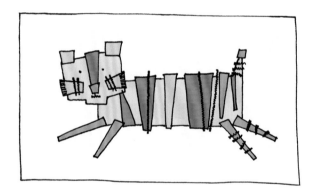

7 Set your sewing machine to a tight zigzag stitch. Make some lines of stitching across the body of the tiger and legs. I chose similar color threads to the fabrics, but really you can choose any colors. Stitch the details on the whiskers and the mouth and use a few small hand stitches on top of each other to make the eyes.

8 Turn under a ¾in (2cm) hem all around the canvas edges and iron in some fusible bonding web to secure. Attach the two bulldog clips. These can be hooked onto a couple of small nails placed on the wall.

LATCH HOOK PILLOW

YOU WILL NEED

- Piece of thick card measuring 5½in (14cm) wide
- Woolen yarn
- Scissors
- Latch hook tool
- Latch hook canvas, 17½ x 17½in (44 x 44cm) square
- Template, page 125
- Two pieces of backing fabric measuring 14½ x 10½in (37 x 27cm) and 14½ x 8in (37 x 20cm)
- Pins
- Needle and cotton sewing thread
- 18in (45cm) pillow pad (this is bigger than the pillow cover but will make a nice plump pillow)

Latch hooking is usually used to make rugs but you can make wonderful, fun, and fluffy pillows using the same method, just on a smaller scale. For me this is the ultimate in mindful craft; it keeps your mind alert but not overly so, and you can let the rhythm of the repeat actions become a very soothing occupation. You do not need a lot of equipment—just a simple latch hook tool, a length of latch hook canvas, and some balls of wool. This project is a great way of using up any scraps of yarn you have in your stash—I love the way you can use different colors and different weights of wool to create something beautifully textural and unique.

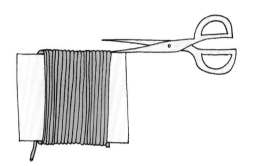

1 Prepare some wool by winding your yarn around the piece of card and cutting top and bottom to make a pile of short lengths of wool.

2 Hold the latch hook in your right hand, or your left hand, if you are left-handed. Take one of your pre-cut pieces of wool and wrap it around the shaft of the latch hook.

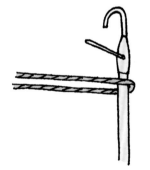

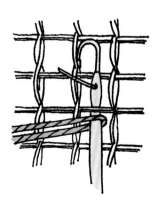

3 Push the end of the latch hook into a hole in the canvas and then out through the hole directly above it. The latch should be open here.

TIP

If you are new to latch hooking, you may find it a good idea to practice using the latch hook and a scrap piece of fabric before you begin the project. Steps 1–5 explain how to hook.

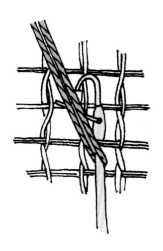

4 Hold the two ends of wool together and position them between the latch and the hook.

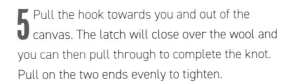

5 Pull the hook towards you and out of the canvas. The latch will close over the wool and you can then pull through to complete the knot. Pull on the two ends evenly to tighten.

6 Now you are ready to start. Draw a 14½in (27cm) square onto your canvas—this is your working square. I have provided a template with suggested areas of color and shape, which you can use for guidance, but really you do not want to be counting squares; it is much better to let the shapes and areas grow organically. It is a lovely way of working that is very freeing.

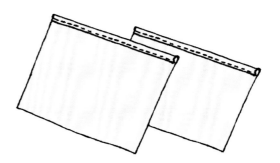

7 When you have finished latch hooking your square, you can now turn it into a pillow cover. Take your two rectangles of backing material and turn over a ½in (1cm) double hem along one long edge on each piece. Pin and stitch in place.

8 Trim the latch canvas back to ¾in (2cm) all around the edge of the worked section and fold in to the edge of the wool section. Fold in a hem on three sides of the rectangle of backing fabric and pin across one end of the pillow. Remember in this case you are pinning the fabric with wrong sides together. Use cotton thread doubled up to hand sew in an overstitch all around three sides.

9 Add the other rectangle at the other end of the pillow in the same way. This rectangle should overlap the first just a little along the sewn hemmed edge. Sew in position. The pillow is ready to fill with the pillow pad.

SKY-BOUND TOWN

YOU WILL NEED

- Templates, page 124
- Tracing paper
- Pencil
- Scissors
- Pins
- Fabric scraps
- Needle and cotton sewing thread
- Fiberfill (polyester stuffing)
- Iron
- Buttons
- 2 lengths of balsa wood measuring ¼ x ¼ x 11in (0.5 x 0.5 x 28cm)
- Wood glue
- ½in (1cm) eyehook

This mobile makes a lovely gift for a first birthday; its fluffy clouds, pretty houses, and little cars adding a charming decoration to any nursery. The small, colorful buttons used for making the wheels on the cars add a supersweet detail.

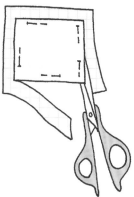

1 To make a little house, trace out a square and a triangle from the templates. Cut out the traces and pin to some fabric. Cut out two of each shape.

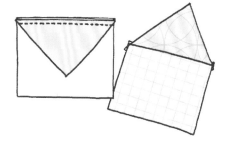

2 With right sides facing, align the base of a triangle with the top of a square. Sew a seam across and trim. Repeat with the two remaining shapes.

3 With right sides facing, place the back and the front of the house together. Pin and sew around the edge, leaving a 1½in (4cm) gap in the seam. Trim the seam and cut across the corners, taking care to avoid any stitches.

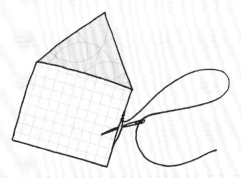

4 Turn the house the right way out and press. Stuff loosely with fiberfill (polyester stuffing).

5 Sew up the gap using small stitches. Repeat the steps to make three more houses. I made two thin-shaped houses and one each of the other sizes.

6 Trace the shape for the tree. Use this to cut back and front tree shapes and sew them together following steps 3, 4, and 5.

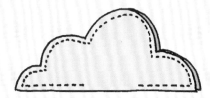

7 Make two clouds in the same way.

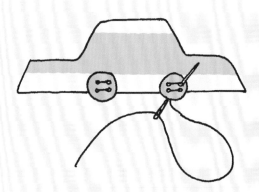

8 Make three cars in the same way. Finish each one with two buttons on each side for the wheels.

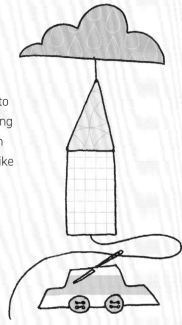

9 Use a needle and thread to sew a car to one of the houses leaving 2in (5cm) gaps between the shapes. Make two like this. Make up another column with a cloud, a house, and a car in the same way.

10 Stitch a loop of thread to the top of each column of shapes and the remaining cloud, house, and tree. Make the loops different lengths.

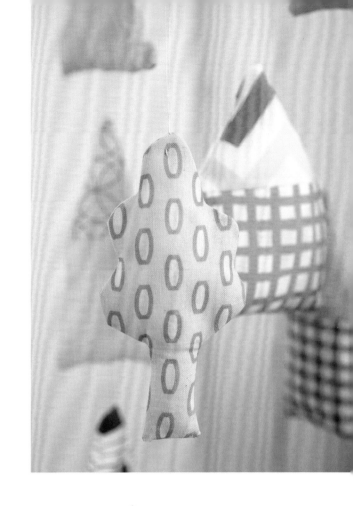

11 Take the two lengths of balsa wood and cross them at the center. Use wood glue to secure the wood where they overlap. Screw an eyehook into the upper strip of wood, at the center.

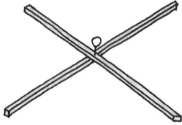

12 Slip the looped threads onto the balsa wood, spreading them out along the four spokes.

13 Tie a length of thread to the eyehook, for hanging. At this point you need to hold the mobile up by the hanging thread to check the balance. You will need to move the looped threads in different directions along the wooden spokes, until the balance is right.

SASHIKO-STITCHED COASTERS

YOU WILL NEED

FOR 1 COASTER

- Two squares of fabric (I used linen), each measuring 7 x 7in (18 x 18cm)
- Ruler
- Set square
- Air- or heat-erasable pen
- Six-stranded embroidery floss (thread)
- Needle (look for special sashiko needles, which are longer than the average needle. I used a regular needle, but picked the longest I had)
- Stitch guide on page 125
- Sewing machine

Embroidery is the perfect way to unwind. I like to have a small piece on the go, to pick up and spend a few quiet moments on when days seem impossibly rushed. I have always been fascinated by the art of Japanese sashiko stitching and have wanted to try it. Sashiko was originally used to reinforce and repair clothing in ancient Japan but it is used as a purely decorative stitch too, with many beautiful and intricate patterns formed from the positioning of small straight stitches. This design is called Hitomezashi Sashiko, where the pattern emerges from lines of single stitches placed on a grid, and is a great way of using up any offcuts of fabric you have from other sewing projects.

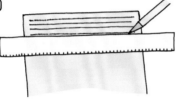

1 Using a set square and ruler, draw a grid on one of the squares of fabric, using an air- or heat-erasable pen. Start the grid ½in (1cm) from the top edge and ½in (1cm) in from the side edge. Space the lines ¼in (5mm) apart. If you draw 24 lines across vertically and horizontally you should have a square grid with a border around it.

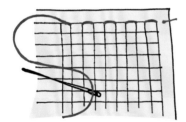

2 Thread a needle with two strands from a length of embroidery floss (thread) and tie a knot at the end. Starting in the top right corner, take the needle down from the front to the back just in the border. Working from right to left, come up at the top corner of the grid. This is your starting point: make a row of running stitches along the line using the grid as a measure and making one stitch per square. Make a few stitches at a time, gathering the fabric on the needle and then pulling the thread through. This will help you to get an even line of stitches.

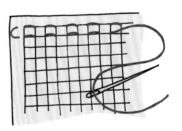

3 When you get to the end, bring the needle out in the border, turn the fabric round, and go back along the second row in the same way, matching the stitches. Always leave a loose loop of thread at the top (don't pull it tight when you stitch the row), as this will stop the stitches from getting tight and not lying flat. If you need to re-thread your needle with new thread it is best to do this at the end of the line, so that you can finish off in the border and start a new line.

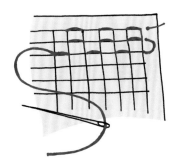

4 On the third line start the row by going down from the front to the back and then up again, so that the first stitch of that row is on the back. Continue along the line. If you follow the stitch guide on page 125 it all becomes very clear as you start stitching.

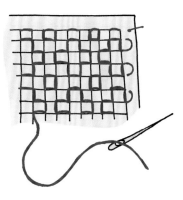

5 The fourth line repeats line three—these four lines make up the pattern. Working in groups of two lines, alternate the stitch position every two lines to continue to the end. Now you repeat the whole thing for the vertical lines. Starting in the top right corner, make your first stitch by going down from the front to the back. Continue stitching as you did on the horizontal lines and you will soon see the pattern emerging.

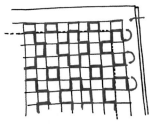

6 When you have finished the stitching, place the back and front pieces with right sides together and pin in position. Sew a line of machine stitches around the grid—I always make the seam one square in. Leave a gap of about 2¾in (7cm) along one edge.

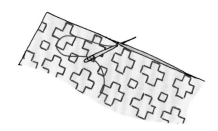

7 Trim back the seam allowance all around to about ⅓in (8mm). Turn the coaster the right way out, fold in the raw edges at the gap, and sew closed with small stitches. Press the coaster. If you used a heat-erasable pen the lines will magically disappear. If you used an air-erasable pen, the lines will fade away.

EMBROIDERED SHIRT

YOU WILL NEED

- Template and stitch guide, page 125
- Tracing paper
- Masking tape
- Old shirt
- Sharp pencil or air-eraseable fabric pen
- Scissors
- Small embroidery hoop (optional)
- Stranded embroidery floss (thread) in assorted colors
- Needle

Transform a plain white shirt into a unique and beautiful item of clothing with some delicate embroidery. With this kind of embroidery, you don't have to follow the pattern to the exact stitch; you may even want to use the outline and fill it in with your own ideas and design. Follow your heart and see what happens. It also doesn't matter if some of your stitch work is a little wobbly—it is all part of the charm and character of handstitched pieces.

1 Transfer the design of the bird from the template on page 125 onto tracing paper.

TIP

I don't often use embroidery hoops as I find it easier without one, but it is a case of preference—you may find that having the fabric pulled taut is helpful.

2 I used a lightbox to transfer the design onto the shirt but if you haven't got a one you can stick the design to the window with some sticky tape and place the shirt over the top. Use a sharp pencil or air-eraseable pen to transfer the design onto the fabric. (Alternatively you could cut out the bird and draw around it, filling in other details by hand.)

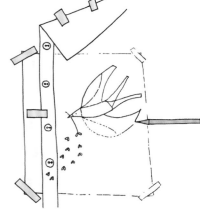

3 Secure the fabric in an embroidery hoop, if using. Start with the outline of the bird: use two strands of embroidery floss (thread) and whipped backstitch to stitch the complete outline of the bird.

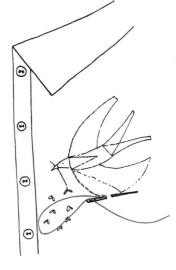

4 Follow the stitch template on page 125 to fill in the design, using whipped backstitch, straight stitch, bullion knots, and detached chain stitches (see the Techniques section on pages 118–119 for more information on how to work these stitches).

TEACUP PINCUSHION

YOU WILL NEED

- Motif and stitch guide on page 125
- Teacup and saucer
- Approximately 8in (20cm) square piece of scrap cotton or linen fabric
- Compass or 7in (18cm) diameter household object
- Air-erasable marker pen
- Dressmaker's carbon paper
- Blue stranded embroidery floss (thread)
- Needle and strong cotton sewing thread
- Fiberfill (polyester stuffing)
- Glue (optional)

I found a set of these cups and saucers in my local thrift store. I love the design, with the charming little folksy scene in blue and pink. It was just right to make into this useful and pretty pincushion, an essential addition to any sewing table. Teacup pincushions are so simple to make and the perfect gift for a crafty friend.

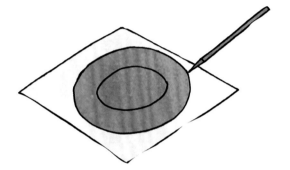

1 My teacup is 3in (8cm) in diameter, if your teacup is smaller adjust the measurements of the circle to fit. Draw a circle onto your fabric with a diameter of 7in (18cm), either using a compass or something round of a similar size, such as a plate or saucepan lid. Cut out the circle.

2 Use dressmaker's carbon paper to transfer the motif on page 125 onto the center of the circle. Follow the stitch guide to embroider the design.

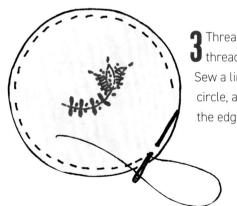

3 Thread a sewing needle with strong cotton thread and double the thread for strength. Sew a line of running stitch all around the circle, approximately ¼in (5mm) in from the edge.

4 Pull the end of the thread so that the circle gathers up into a ball shape. When the opening is approximately 2in (5cm) wide, tie off the end of the thread. Stuff the circle with small amounts of stuffing until you have a nice firm ball.

5 Push the pincushion down into the cup until it is firmly in place. You can glue it into position if you like.

TECHNIQUES

ADHESIVES

I use different types of glue for different projects, as well as a selection of adhesive tapes. When using glue sticks, try to find one with clear glue because this type never seems to clog up. Craft glue is white when it goes on but dries clear and is a very good adhesive for large areas. Use a brush or a small piece of card stock (card) to apply it. Strong, quick-drying glue is clear and usually comes in a tube. You will also need several types of adhesive tape, for instance: masking tape, double-sided tape, and washi tape.

TRACING

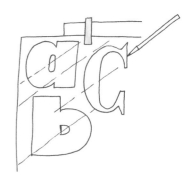

For many projects you need to transfer the template onto paper or card stock (card), using tracing paper. Place a sheet of tracing paper over the template and secure with some masking tape. Trace the lines with a hard 4 (2H) pencil, then turn the tracing paper over and go over the lines again on the reverse with a softer pencil, such as a 2 (HB). Now turn the tracing paper over again and place it in position on your chosen paper or card stock (card). Go over all the lines carefully with the 4 (2H) pencil, and then remove the tracing paper. This will give you a nice, clear outline.

CUTTING

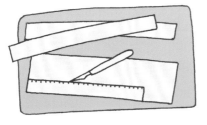

I use a scalpel or craft knife for nearly all my projects. Make sure the blade is sharp and that you always use a cutting mat. When you need to make a straight cut, use a metal ruler and keep the blade in contact with the ruler at all times. Cut toward you, maintaining an even pressure.

SCORING

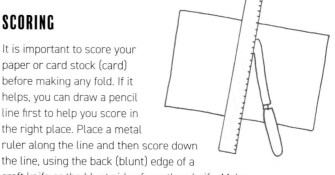

It is important to score your paper or card stock (card) before making any fold. If it helps, you can draw a pencil line first to help you score in the right place. Place a metal ruler along the line and then score down the line, using the back (blunt) edge of a craft knife or the blunt side of a cutlery knife. Make sure you keep the side of the blade in contact with the ruler.

HAND-SEWING SKILLS

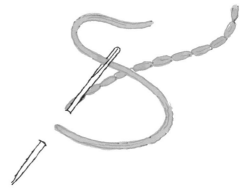

Running stitch

Work from right to left. Secure the thread with a couple of small stitches, and then make several small stitches by bringing the needle up and back down through the fabric several times along the stitching line. Pull the needle through and repeat. Try to keep the stitches and the spaces between them the same size.

Backstitch

Work from right to left. Bring the needle up from the back of the fabric, one stitch length to the left of the end of the stitching line. Insert it one stitch length to the right, at the very end of the stitching line, and bring it up again one stitch length in front of the point from which it first emerged. Pull the thread through. To begin the next stitch, insert the needle at the left-hand end of the previous stitch. Continue to the end.

Straight stitch

Bring the needle through to the surface of the fabric and then take it back down to create a small straight stitch. These can be worked at random or as part of a design.

Seed stitch

Work pairs of very short straight stitches, positioning them randomly to fill an area.

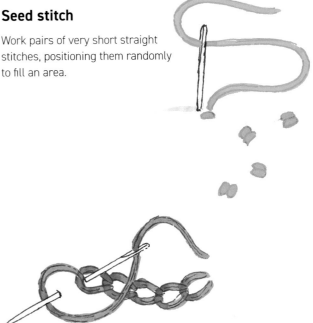

Whipped backstitch

Work a line of backstitches (see page 118). Using a blunt needle, slide the needle under the thread of the first backstitch from top to bottom and pull the thread through. Repeat in each stitch in the row.

Chain stitch

Bring the needle out at the end of the stitching line. Re-insert it at the same point and bring it out a short distance away, looping the thread around the needle tip. Pull the thread through. To begin the next stitch, insert the needle at the point at which it last emerged, just inside the loop of the previous chain, and bring it out a short distance away, again looping the thread around the needle tip. Repeat to continue.

Detached chain stitch

Work a single chain (see right), but fasten it by taking a small vertical stitch across the bottom of the loop.

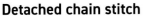

French knot

Bring the needle up from the back of the fabric to the front. Wrap the thread two or three times around the tip of the needle, then re-insert the needle at the point where it first emerged, holding the wrapped threads with the thumbnail of your non-stitching hand, and pull the needle all the way through. The wraps will form a knot on the surface of the fabric.

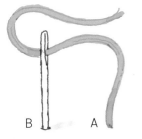

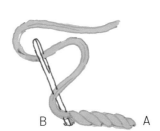

B   A   B   A   B   A

Bullion knot

This is similar to a French knot, but creates a longer coil of thread rather than a single knot. Bring the needle up at A and take it down at B, leaving a loose loop of thread—the distance from A to B being the length of knot that you require. Bring the needle back up at A and wrap the thread around the needle five to eight times, depending on how long you want the knot to be.

Hold the wrapped thread in place with your left hand and pull the needle all the way through. Insert the needle at B and pull through, easing the coiled stitches neatly into position. Check each template to see what size bullion knot is required for each project.

TEMPLATES

ENLARGING TEMPLATES

Some of the templates on pages 120–125 will need to be enlarged. Each template is clearly marked at the percentage of actual size that it is printed, so you will need to enlarge it to the size it is to be used at. If a template is 50% of actual size, then it is half of its actual size and will need to be enlarged by 200% on a photocopier. The appliqué wall hanging template on page 122 is shown at 25%, which means that it is a quarter of its actual size and will need to be increased by 400% (four times its size). To do this, enlarge by 200% on a photocopier, and then enlarge that photocopy by another 200%.

TRANSFERRING PATTERNS AND MOTIFS

For some of the fabric projects, you will need to transfer an embroidery pattern or motif onto the fabric. I use three different methods.

The first—and the easiest—is tracing. If the fabric is sheer enough, lay it over the pattern and trace it, using a dressmaker's fade-away marker pen. Alternatively, tape the pattern to a window with the fabric on top, and draw over the lines of the pattern.

The second method is for thick or dark fabrics. Lay dressmaker's carbon paper on the fabric, carbon side down. Lay the embroidery pattern on top and trace over the motif with a ballpoint pen. You can buy carbon paper in different colors suitable for different fabrics.

The final method is for the few fabrics that have a fluffy pile and are difficult to draw on. Trace the motif onto a piece of white tissue paper and pin it onto the fabric. Using cotton sewing thread and a closely spaced running stitch, baste (tack) through the tissue paper and fabric along the pattern lines. Remove the tissue paper, complete the embroidery, and then remove the basting (tacking) stitches.

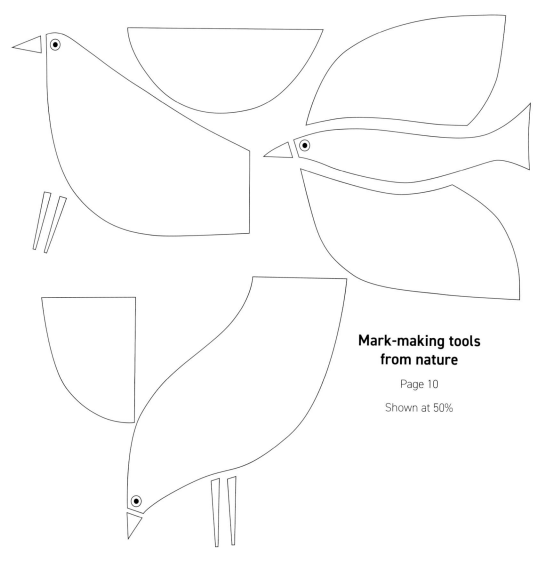

**Mark-making tools
from nature**

Page 10

Shown at 50%

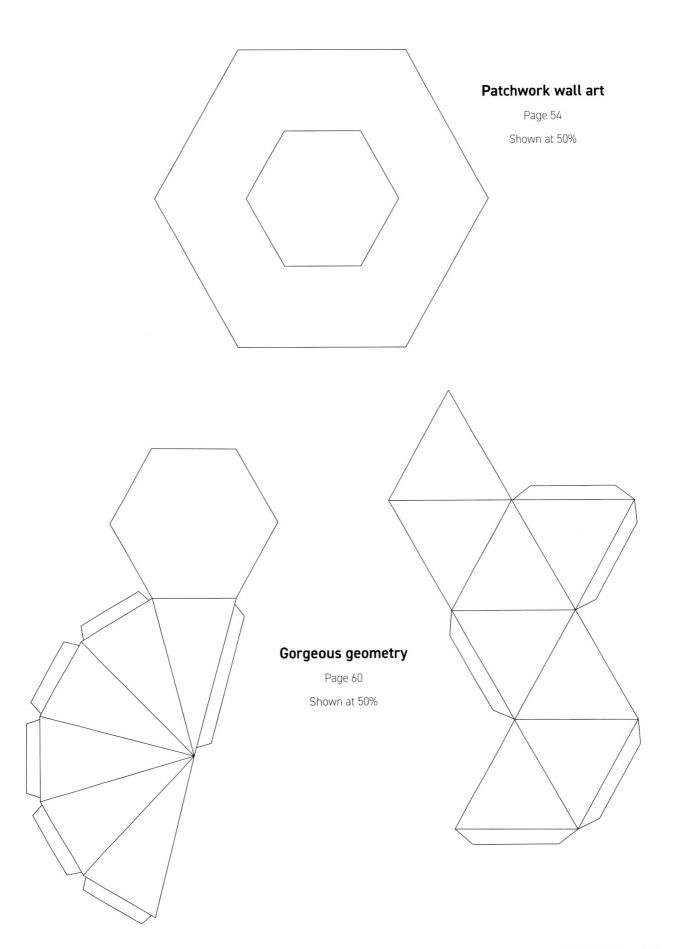

Patchwork wall art

Page 54

Shown at 50%

Gorgeous geometry

Page 60

Shown at 50%

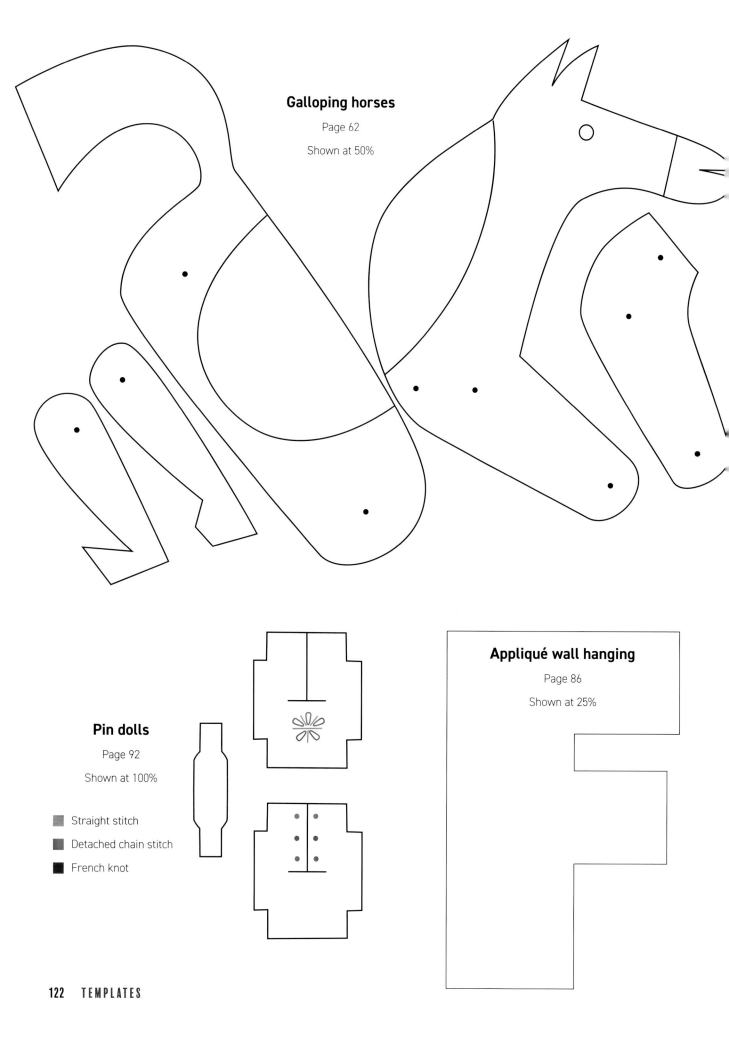

Galloping horses

Page 62

Shown at 50%

Appliqué wall hanging

Page 86

Shown at 25%

Pin dolls

Page 92

Shown at 100%

Straight stitch

Detached chain stitch

French knot

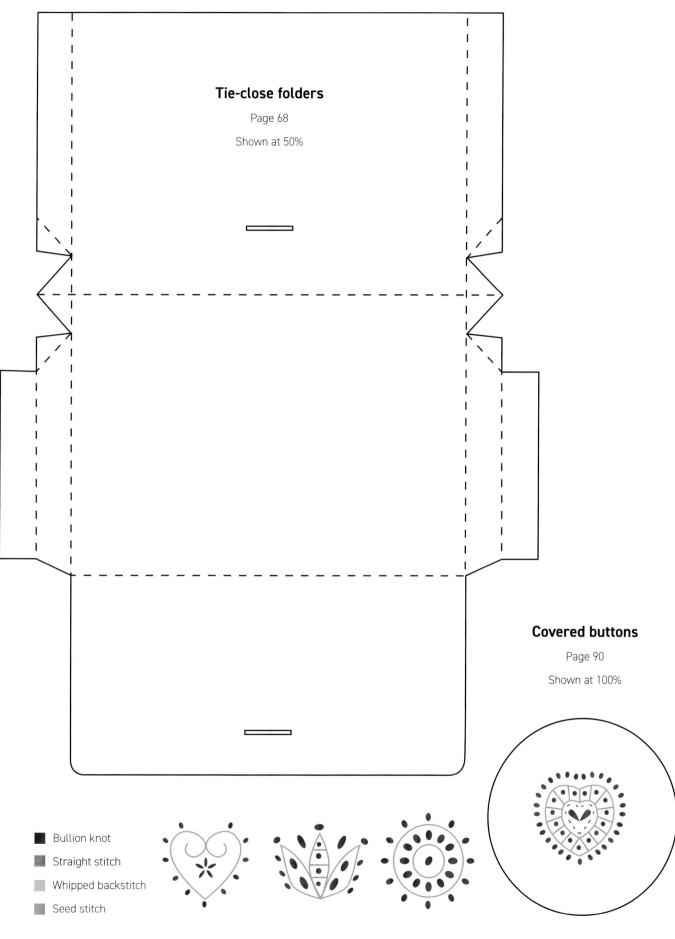

Tie-close folders

Page 68

Shown at 50%

Covered buttons

Page 90

Shown at 100%

Bullion knot

Straight stitch

Whipped backstitch

Seed stitch

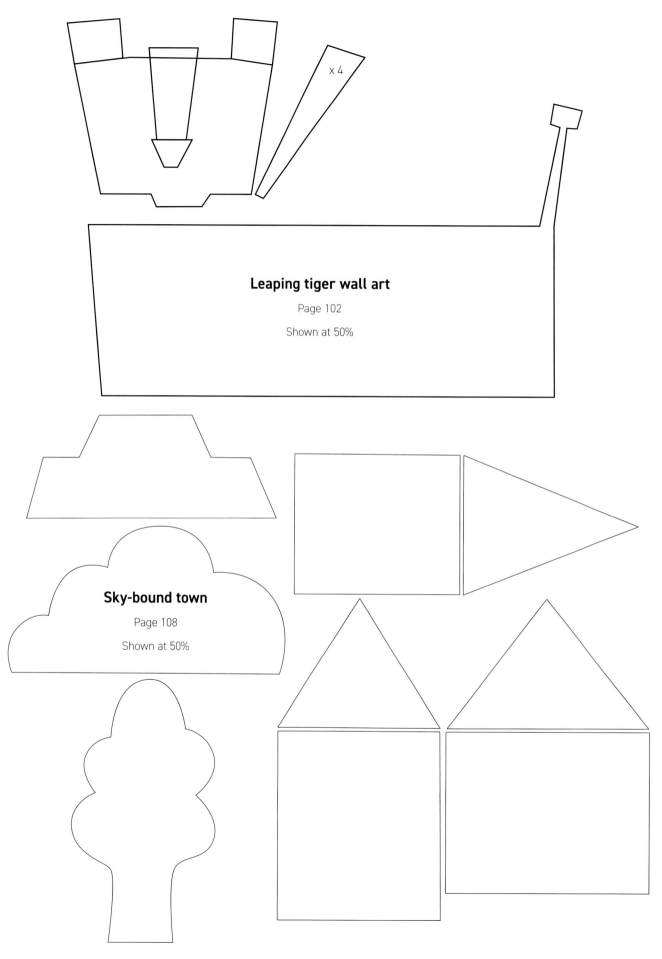

Leaping tiger wall art

Page 102

Shown at 50%

Sky-bound town

Page 108

Shown at 50%

x 4

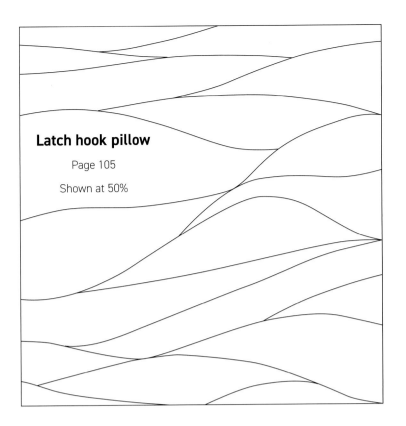

Latch hook pillow

Page 105

Shown at 50%

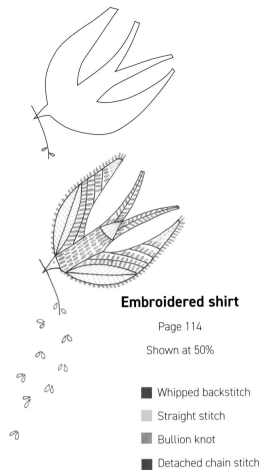

Embroidered shirt

Page 114

Shown at 50%

■ Whipped backstitch

▨ Straight stitch

■ Bullion knot

■ Detached chain stitch

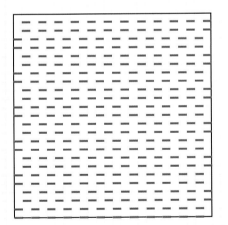

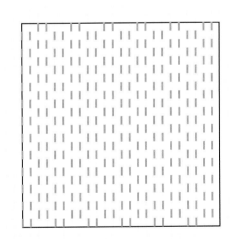

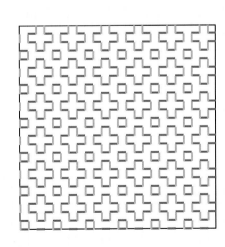

Sashiko-stitched coasters

Page 112

Shown at 50%

Teacup pincushion

Page 116

Shown at 100%

■ Bullion knot

■ Straight stitch

■ Backstitch

SUPPLIERS

US stockists

Hobby Lobby
www.hobbylobby.com

Jo-Ann Fabric and Craft Store
www.joann.com

Michaels
www.michaels.com

UK stockists

Cass Art
www.cassart.co.uk

Cloth House
www.clothhouse.com

Crafty Devils
www.craftydevilspapercraft.co.uk

Hobbycraft
www.hobbycraft.co.uk

John Lewis
www.johnlewis.com

Paperchase
www.paperchase.com

INDEX

ACKNOWLEDGMENTS

I have been very lucky to work on some lovely craft books in the last few years and this one is no exception. I would like to say a big thank you to CICO Books for giving me the opportunity to put this collection of projects together on a subject that is so close to my heart. Thanks to all the team at CICO Books, especially Jenny Dye, Sally Powell, Penny Craig, and Patricia Harrington who are always such a pleasure to work with. Thank you to Joanna Henderson, Caroline Arber, and James Gardiner for the wonderful photography. Also to the memory of Claire Richardson, a brilliant photographer and such a good friend. I have cherished memories of the times we worked together. Thanks to Kate Hardwicke, Anna Southgate, and Clare Sayer for their careful and considered editing. Thank you to Geoff Borin for the stylish design. Finally, thank you Ian for your lovely artworks but mostly for always being there for me.